Phil Polley

THE PITCH

HUGH RANK

THE COUNTER — PROPAGANDA PRESS
PARK FOREST, ILLINOIS 60466
1982

Copyright © 1982 by Hugh Rank
First Edition
Printed in the United States of America

Published by
The Counter-Propaganda Press
Park Forest, Illinois 60466

Library of Congress Cataloging in Publication Data

Rank, Hugh D., 1932-
The Pitch
includes index
1. Advertising.   I. Title.
HF5821.R26   1982   659.1   82-8107
ISBN 0-943468-00-0   AACR2

Acknowledgements

The author wishes to thank the following for permission to reproduce material in this book:

Crain Communications, Inc. for the statistical data on advertising expenditures as reprinted form *Advertising Age.*

Excerpt from *The Best Thing on TV* by Jonathan Price.
Copyright © 1978 by Jonathan Price. Reprinted by permission of Viking Press Inc.

James Harvey Young, *The Toadstool Millionaires: A Social History of Patent Medicine in America Before Federal Regulation* Copyright © 1961 by Princeton University Press. Excerpt, pp. 195-6, reprinted by permission of Princeton University Press.

The author wishes especially to acknowledge the help of his students at Governors State University whose aid and encouragement, insight and efforts are greatly appreciated.

dedicated to

Elizabeth, Christopher, James-Jonathan, David

my own kids,
and to their generation,
now coming of age —

Be disillusioned, but not discouraged:
Lose your illusions, but not your courage.

Contents

CONTENTS

THE BLITZ 9

    Propaganda as "organized persuasion"
        as "growth industry"

    Counter-Propaganda & Advertising Analysis

    Benefit-Seeking & Benefit-Promising

1 ATTENTION-GETTING (HI) 19

    Cutting through the Clutter

    Physical Attention-Getters

    Emotional Attention-Getters

    Cognitive Attention-Getters
        — *News*   — *Questions*
        — *Lists & Displays*   — *Stories*
        — *Claims & Promises*   — *Demonstrations*
        — *Advice*   — *Breaking Rules*
        — *Lead-ins*   — *Humor*

2 CONFIDENCE-BUILDING (TRUST ME) 31

    The Image *(ethos)*
    — expert
    — sincere
    — benevolent

    Authority Figures & Friend Figures

    Trademarks & Brand Names

    The "Personal Touch" with Computers

3 DESIRE-STIMULATING (YOU NEED) 41

    Old & New: Product-Oriented & Audience-Oriented Ads

    Benefit-Seeking: Four Basic Behaviors

    Persuaders as Benefit-Promisers: Basic Behaviors

    Intrinsic Merits of Products: Claims & Promises 49
        — *Superiority*   — *Stability*
        — *Quantity*   — *Reliability*
        — *Beauty*   — *Simplicity*
        — *Efficiency*   — *Utility*
        — *Scarcity*   — *Rapidity*
        — *Novelty*   — *Safety*

    Most Commonly Repeated Advertising Claims 74

    Needs, Wants, & Desires: A Useful List 76

    "Added Values" Suggested by Association Techniques

        Manipulating Human Hopes and Fears, Dreams and Nightmares

        Common Categories of Needs/Wants/Desires 82
          — *Food*   — *Religion*   — *Intimacy*
          — *Activity*   — *Science*   — *Family*
          — *Surroundings*   — *Elite* ("Best People")   — *Belonging*
          — *Sex*   — *Popularity* ("Most")   — *Esteem*
          — *Health*   — *Normality* ("Average")   — *Play*
          — *Security*   — *Neighborhood*   — *Generosity*
          — *Economy*   — *Nation*   — *Curiosity*
               — *Nature*   — *Creativity*
                             — *Completion*

    Some Standard Phrasings in Ads

Contents 7

4 URGENCY-STRESSING (HURRY) 133

   Command Propaganda

   Conditioning Propaganda

      — "Soft Sell," "Image Building" Ads, PR

   Common Situations: "Hard Sell" & "Soft Sell" 137

5 RESPONSE-SEEKING (BUY) 141

   Response as Goal

   Triggering Words

   Mass Media Response Devices

THE 30-SECOND SPOT QUIZ 147

   Suggestions: How To Analyze Ads

   The Quick 1-2-3-4-5 Overview

THE INTENSIFY/DOWNPLAY SCHEMA 151

QUESTIONS YOU CAN ASK ABOUT ANY AD 155

REFERENCE GUIDE:
ADS FOR COMMON PRODUCTS & SERVICES 158

Soft Drinks	Cars	Self-Improvement
Beer	Car Care	Get-Rich-Quick
Liquor	Motorcycles	
Cigarettes	Cameras	Real Estate
Candy	Stereos	Home Repairs
Cereals	LP Records	Furniture & Appliances
Snack Foods	Entertainments	Utilities
Easy-Foods	Hotels/Motels	Insurance
Fast-Foods	Airlines	Baby Care
O-T-C Drugs		Toys
	Military	Cleaning Aids
"Body Work"	College	Banks
Cosmetics	Job	Credit Cards
Clothes	Wedding	Funerals

ADVERTISING EXPENDITURES 200

ABOUT THE AUTHOR 203

INDEX 205

This book will show you **how** to analyze ads. This chapter will tell you **why** it's important and useful to develop this skill. ▶

If you've ever felt...
manipulated by advertisers, politicians, and other public persuaders;
irritated at *what* they say, or at *how* they say it;
exasperated because "something's wrong";
frustrated because it's hard to pinpoint the problem;
bored by constant repetition;
bothered by deliberate omission;
deceived by cleverly-worded phrases;
betrayed by misplaced confidence;
dissatisfied with what you *got* for what you *gave;*
disappointed in claims overstated and promises not kept;
annoyed by the vulgarity;
insulted by the simplicity;
confused by the complexity;
overwhelmed by the chaos;
read on. This book's for you.

THE BLITZ

These *feelings* are understandable, even though these complaints may be overstated. A real problem does exist within our society: we often encounter widespread feelings of such cynicism, mistrust, suspicion, free-floating anger, and disillusionment about the messages we see and hear on television and radio, in the newspapers and magazines.

We're living in the midst of the most intense, most sophisticated propaganda blitz in human history. In our daily environment we are subjected to more persuasion attempts than ever generated in the supposedly "classic" propaganda campaigns of Nazi Germany. During the past generation, a serious problem of *inequality* has developed between the average person and the "professional persuaders." As an individual, you need to know more about propaganda techniques to protect yourself.

"Propaganda," as used here, means *organized persuasion:* commercial advertising, "public relations" by business and corporations, "publicity" efforts by a wide variety of "good causes," special interest groups, religious organizations, political parties, and governmental sources. No matter what the subject matter — consumer products, political and governmental policies, social and religious ideas — such organized persuasion is big business. Propaganda is a "growth industry" in the world today.

Growth can be measured in terms of dollars spent, and the quantity and frequency of messages sent: *how much, how many, how often?*

Advertising expenditures, for example, in one decade soared from $19.5 billion in 1970 to $54.6 billion in 1980, totaling more than $362.5 billion for that period. Over 42,000 *new* TV commercials are developed each year, adding to the hundreds of thousands already made. Some estimates claim the average American child sees 100,000 commercials before being old enough to go to school. In 1981, a Cap'n Crunch cereal contest, unnoticed by most adults, asked kids to respond by using an 800 phone number; in 4 months, the Captain and his crew were overwhelmed by 24 million phonecalls. Such gee-whiz statistics can only suggest the scope of advertising's impact on our society.

Senator William Fulbright's *The Pentagon Propaganda Machine,* in 1970, cited awesome statistics showing that governmental expenditures for domestic "information" *to persuade its own people* were more than double the combined costs of the major newsgathering organizations (the wire services, TV networks, and major newspapers). Today, such self-serving promotional activities continue to expand; budget cut-backs seldom affect such "informational" programs.

Even religious persuasion is a booming industry. By 1981 (according to Charles Swann, author of *Prime-Time Preachers*), there were over 100 evangelical preachers who had TV programs syndicated on more than five stations. Furthermore, on *thousands* of radio stations throughout the country, such persuaders (aided now by WATS lines and computerized direct mailings) are not only preaching, but also asking for a few dollars to help "spread the word."

However, it's not only growth, but it's also *change* that's been happening recently. Never before has persuasion been so smooth, slick, and sophisticated, nor delivered so quickly to so many people. People have *always* tried to persuade others. Some persuaders have *always* been more skillful, more aware, more able, more interested, or better trained than others. But, in the past, this natural inequality was *limited:* only a rare person had the memory, intelligence, wit, and skills of strategy to be an effective persuader, and such abilities died with the person. Today, computers can store massive amounts of information, retrieve it instantly, sort it for use according to pre-set plans. Such systematic tools, together with money, media access, research abilities, and organized work teams are available now to the professional persuaders. **This situation of inequality is a problem.**

Some people see *no problem* with this fantastic growth, change, and concentration of organized persuasion. Some people see no bad effects, no immediate or possible threat, to themselves or their group. Or they minimize the degree: "it's *not much* of a problem." They assume *benevolence* and *altruism* on the part of the powerful.

Some people assume *existing counter-measures* are already built into the system, that government regulatory agencies are adequately protecting the citizens, and that schools are adequately preparing their children. Or they assume that people need not be trained, that children need not be taught the techniques of persuasion; such analytical and critical skills are expected to develop *naturally,* by experience, or, perhaps, by osmosis.

Some people simply don't recognize the problem. It's so hard to grasp such an abstract situation. Advertising statistics, for example, are as mind-boggling, remote, and unreal as the federal budget: How does one *comprehend* the concept that it costs nearly a half-million dollars to air a 30-second TV spot during the Super Bowl game? What does $60 billion dollars mean?

The growing imbalance is also obscured by the abundance of technological inventions *commonly shared* by both persuaders and persuadees. For instance, the average household today is filled with sophisticated electronic hardware unimaginable a lifetime ago: color TV, hi-fi, transistor radios, videogames, computer terminals. Message receivers, especially young people, are likely to be very adept at handling the hardware of things which were miracles yesterday, commonplaces today. But, far fewer people understand the inner operations and the software, if this term can be used to suggest the various strategies and tactics involved in composing the messages to be transmitted.

Furthermore, the problem is obscured because a *situation* of inequality does not have a necessary, direct, and specific *cause-and-effect* relationship with any bad results. Simply because such sophisticated persuasion techniques are concentrated in the hands of a few does *not necessarily* mean that such power will be abused or that others will be harmed. Conditions are not causes. It would be much easier to understand and to counteract a specific cause!

However, wise people also take precautions about *conditions* or *circumstances* which are potentially dangerous. By analogy, Midwesterners are accustomed to "tornado alerts," warnings that the weather conditions are favorable for tornadoes to develop. Such warnings alert both individuals and communities to take precautions such as training the children, building shelters, and having relief plans ready. Tornadoes may be hard to predict and impossible to stop, but we do try to protect ourselves by our own alertness when conditions are ripe. Conditions are ripe today for a propaganda blitz unparalleled in human history.

Governments and their functionaries, political parties and their leaders, corporations and their products, are always making claims and promises, begging for our belief and confidence in them: "Trust me" is the standard plea of every politician and every product peddled.

Our dilemma is that we cannot survive if we believe *everything,* nor can we survive if we don't believe *anything.* On one hand, there's a danger of us believing everything: being ignorant, naive, gullible, docile, unaware of the problems, of being exploited and victimized. On the other hand, there's the problem of believing *nothing:* of being overly suspicious, paranoid, bitter, cynical, blaming others for all problems, and imagining secret conspiracies, hidden persuaders, and subliminal seducers making us do things against our will. As *receivers* of messages, we need a more realistic moderate position avoiding these extremes. A common sense sanity and practicality, an attitude of healthy skepticism.

In our daily person-to-person communications, most people *do* avoid the extremes. We know, for example, that different people can be trusted, or not trusted, in varying degrees. From experience, we gradually make these judgments about our friends and acquaintances. But, the *mutuality* and *equality* in such close contacts is missing in our relationship with the professional persuaders in the mass media.

Organized persuasion is not intrinsically evil: the people involved, their motives and the results, may be either "good" or "bad." But this growing *inequality* and lack of mutuality between the professional persuaders and the average persuadees creates a great potential danger.

An important new survival skill in the modern world will be our ability to analyze such propaganda, to make critical judgments, to transform our vague feelings of trust or district into specific acceptance or rejection. Ideally, we would seek to judge political issues and commercial products on their own merits rather than on the cleverness of the persuader.

Counter-Propaganda is needed. Not against a particular group or idea, but some kind of counter-balancing on behalf of *individuals* against *any* of the professional persuaders: commercial or political, Left or Right or Anywhere Else, church or corporation, "good guys" or "bad guys," whatever the Cause, whoever the Speaker.

This book is counter-propaganda. It will show *you,* as the target of many persuaders, how to cope better with the blitz. Specifically, it will show you how to analyze advertising, the most visible and obvious form of such organized persuasion. If you agree there's a fantastic increase in the amount and sophistication of propaganda, then it makes sense to consider our own counter-measures, simply on the traditional basis that "forewarned is forearmed" ("praemunitas, praemonitas"). Others are trying to sell us their products or their policies; such persuasion involves not only how we spend our money, but also how we spend our time, our lives.

Advertising may not be the most important aspect of modern propaganda; obviously, the ultimate problems of our age relate to nuclear war, pollution of the planet, and survival of the species. But, such problems are often so complex, abstract, seemingly remote, emotionally fraught and unthinkable, that they may be very difficult places to start analyzing persuasion techniques.

Advertising analysis is the best starting point for a better understanding of *all* persuasion. Ads are often the best *composition* of our age, skillful combinations of purposeful words and images. Furthermore, ads are easily available in great quantity and variety, are frequently interesting or entertaining, and are a common denominator in our society.

Ads, in themselves, may not be important. But *your mind* is. If we can better learn how to analyze things, to recognize patterns, to sort out incoming information, to see the parts, the processes, the structure, the relationships within things so common in our everyday environment, then it's worth the effort we make. Certainly, any skills learned, any insights gained can be transferred to the analysis of other things.

Using advertising is the easiest way to start analyzing propaganda; using *The Pitch* is the easiest way to start analyzing advertising. This book is a *new* application of some *traditional* concepts of rhetoric, presenting some plain talk and common sense advice on how to analyze persuasion. This book will focus your attention on some key items and give you the tools for analysis: a *method,* a *pattern* and a *working vocabulary.*

With these tools, you will be able to transform vague feelings into specific statements, and to change random comments into a systematic analysis. Using *The Pitch,* as an organizing principle, you can anticipate incoming information. You'll have some *way* to sort, some *place* to store. If you know the common patterns of persuasion, you can pick up cues from bits and fragments, recognize the situation, know the probable options, infer the rest, and even note the omissions. After reading *The Pitch,* you'll be better able to understand the techniques not only of advertisers, but also of all persuaders. You'll know better what to expect in the *form* and *content* of the messages, and the *behaviors* of the persuaders.

This book is *not* a "hatchet job" against advertising. The assumption here is everyone, in a free society, has the right to try to persuade others in a fair and honest exchange. Advertising is *not* seen as a conspiracy against the consumer, but as the corporation's way of stimulating the demand for those products which can be supplied, efficiently, at a profit to the producer. This book is *not* a diatribe about deceptive advertising, hard-core fraud or even borderline cases. But, it is about the common, ordinary, true-as-far-as-they-go ads of our everyday experiences.

Randomness characterizes most discussions and books about advertising. If you've ever discussed advertising with friends, at a party, or in school, you'll recall how frequently the conversation jumps around: from products and slogans, to actors and actresses; from expressions of personal likes and dislikes, to arguments about the morality, the legality, the honesty, or the effectiveness of advertising. It's very hard to carry on a sustained coherent conversation about advertising because of such sidetracking and shifting premises. Most books about advertising are as haphazard, usually relating fragmentary anecdotes about specific ad campaigns or individual advertisers. Much has already been said and written about advertising, both by advocates and by critics. While it is perfectly valid to discuss advertising from any number of ways, be aware of the approach used. Consider these basic questions: *who is saying what, to whom, when and where, with what intent, with what result, and how.*

Some analysts are most concerned with *who,* that is, a focus on the advertisers ("Madison Avenue"), or, in the case of political persuasion, a focus on the government (the Pentagon, the White House). Whether it's advertiser or politician, clergyman or educator, reformer or huckster, some people are most concerned with the *source* of the message, the *speaker.*

Other people focus on the *audience;* that is, *to whom* is the message being sent. Audiences can be categorized in many ways: according to age, sex, race, affluence (or the lack of it), sophistication (or the lack of it), location, etc. Obviously, some audiences are more vulnerable than others. Some critics are very concerned about the influence of advertising upon children, young women, on blacks, on latinos, on the poor, on the farmer, on foreign audiences, and so on.

The *context* of advertising is sometimes discussed: the time and place factors, *when* and *where.* Usually, context is considered in terms of *appropriateness* and *effectiveness.* Liquor and cigarette ads, for example, are not permitted in some places. Certain television commercials might be inappropriate or ineffective with some programs, at some times during the day, and so on.

Much attention has already been given to *what* is being said: the content, or substance, of both the explicit and implicit messages being sent. Some people object to specific *products* being advertised: laxatives, deodorants, toilet paper, tampons, condoms, sanitary napkins, bras, and panty hose. Some people believe these products are, or should be, the *"unmentionables."* Anything to do with bodily functions (sex, excretion, menstruation) is considered *"distasteful", "offensive," "vulgar," "crude," "suggestive," "morally harmful."* Other people object to other products (beer, cigarettes, sugared cereals, sleeping pills) because they believe these to be *"dangerous," "unhealthy,"* or *"harmful"* to both the individual and the society.

Others object to the *implied messages,* the general tone and attitude of advertising which encourages greed and gluttony, pleasure-seeking and permissiveness. Such advertising, critics claim, sends the messages that happiness can be bought, and that every desire should be gratified, as quickly as possible, by buying something. Some people see advertising as immoral economic exploitation, harmful to middle-class families caught up in a debt cycle, devastating to very poor. Other people object to what they see as a world of uniformity, mediocrity, conformity and sameness because of the close ties between advertising and mass-production. Others object to advertising as insulting their intelligence, a world of simplistic ideas, simple solutions, and annoying repetitions, geared at a twelve-year old mentality.

Others object to advertising as harmful to the mental health of the individual and the whole society: ads create a world of hype, of illusions, of unrealistic expectations — and, subsequently, of disappointment and frustration when these expectations cannot be met. Other people object to sexist advertising presenting false images of women, perpetuating sexist myths, or treating women as sex objects. Other people complain about racist implications, usually that certain ethnic groups are being omitted from ads or are not being presented favorably. For many reasons, critics attack advertising for its *content.*

Discussions of the *consequences* or *effects* of advertising are often closely linked with discussions of the *intent or motives* of the persuaders: *why?* The most obvious reason is that the persuader seeks to gain a benefit: advertisers seek profit; politicians, power. So also, the most obvious reason why the audience responds is that people seek to gain a benefit for themselves. They buy, vote, or act in their own self-interest. A product may mean *profit* to the corporation, but *pleasure* to the consumer.

Critics often attack advertisers, charging that some ads are *deliberately* deceptive, or *intentionally* misleading and other kinds of "mind-reading" statements. The accused advertisers can either *claim innocence* (accidental, unconscious, unintentional, mistakes, errors) or can *defend their actions* based on righteous motives: needed product, bringer of pleasure and hope; free enterprise, individual liberty, freedom of choice. (It is a very complex problem to judge other peoples' motives. But, if we assume that everyone can defend and justify their own motives as being right, then it's often more useful to judge the *consequences* to ourselves and to society.)

Other writers about advertising have emphasized "hidden persuaders" and "subliminal seduction" in analyzing some of the psychological strategies used by advertisers. Some of their ideas have led, unwittingly, to an undue suspicion that advertisers have irresistible secret weapons which can overwhelm us, or a kind of conspiracy theory that advertisers are out to get us. Such attitudes encourage easy excuses: people claiming non-responsibility, that they can't help themselves because they were brainwashed by the "bad guys out there." Such scapegoating diverts attention away from recognizing our own desires, our own choices, and our own responsibility.

Advertisers can not make us do anything we don't already want to do. However, they can try to channel our existing desires for their own ends. Sometimes this is beneficial to both parties, sometimes not. One way to protect our own interests is to start with some realistic premises about our own desires.

Awareness of our own benefit-seeking is our primary defense against the professional persuaders. We can little control what the persuaders do, but we can control ourselves. By conscious choice, we can order our own priorities. Our goals (the benefits we seek) are linked with our beliefs (what we think, what we value), our emotions (how we feel), and our behaviors (what we do).

Most persuasion isn't hidden. We simply have to recognize our own behavior as benefit-seekers, and some of the common patterns used by the benefit-promisers.

In brief, this book emphasizes two important things: (1) the basic premise that human beings are *benefit-seekers;* (2) the most common pattern used by advertisers as benefit-promisers — *"the pitch."*

Benefit-Seekers. So what? To say that people are *benefit-seekers* is so vague and general that it's to the point of being a "ho-hum" truism. So what? What's new?

But, if we can *specify* and *categorize* some three dozen kinds of *benefits,* and specify their *opposites* (the fears, the nightmares used in "scare-and-sell" ads), list and group together hundreds of specific *words* and *images* and dramatized *scenes* used today in persuasion, then the concept of benefit-seeking ceases to be a meaningless generalization. We'll recognize not only the *overall patterns,* but also where all the *parts relate.* In the core chapter ("You Need"), these concepts are more fully explained as these categories and lists are presented. Furthermore, the book emphasizes the basic dynamics of our own benefit-seeking and the basic patterns of benefit-promising by the persuaders.

Forewarned *is* forearmed. Knowing these things helps us understand propaganda, anticipate what's coming, and sort out the complexities. Such knowledge helps us protect ourselves. Most of us learn these things, eventually, by trial and error. But, that's a slow, haphazard, and, often costly, way. Here's a quick and simple way we can learn how to protect ourselves by knowing some basics about persuasion.

To simplify a complex process, the term "the pitch" will be used here to describe the most common pattern of persuasion found in commercial advertising.

"The pitch" is an old American slang term, variously defined as "a set talk designed to persuade" (*American Heritage Dictionary*); "an often high-pressure sales talk; advertisement" *(Webster's New Collegiate)*; "a line of talk, such as a salesman uses to persuade customers" *(Webster's New World)*. Now, "the pitch" is my term for describing a five-part strategy as the *basic pattern* of persuasion in that large quantity of advertising emphasizing *non-rational* elements.

Using the pattern of "the pitch" is the *easiest way* to analyze ads: a fingertip 1-2-3-4-5 sequence, easy to memorize, simple to use, complete here with cartoon balloons; yet, sophisticated, elegant, and accurate. Some people will recognize that "the pitch" is akin to the traditional pattern emphasizing *rational* persuasion, the classical oration *(exordium, narration, confirmation, refutation, peroration)*. Other formulas (such as "AIDA") and other analyses (such as Monroe's "Motivated Sequence") have focused on the patterns of persuasion in advertising. But none are as complete and systematic, nor designed for the *receivers* of the messages: the average citizen and consumer.

Qualifications will be made, and variations will be shown throughout the book, but start off by recognizing that the *superstructure* of this book is the five-part pattern of "the pitch":

1. Attention-getting

2. Confidence-building

3. Desire-stimulating

4. Urgency-stressing

5. Response-seeking

1

ATTENTION-GETTING

Hundreds of thousands of ads compete for our attention. Today, over 42,000 *new* TV commercials are produced each year, making up only a small portion of the total number of ads we see and hear. Billions of dollars are spent on a process of persuasion in which a very critical step is the initial point of contact between the persuader and the audience. The first part of "the pitch" is the *attention-getter: Hi!*

You can't persuade if no one's listening or watching.

First, an ad has to get attention; *finally,* an effective ad has to get response. But *first,* an ad has to be heard or seen.

"The greatest sin in advertising," as one wit said, "is not to be noticed," a paraphrase of that cynical comment, "There's no such thing as *bad* publicity." People may hate certain TV commercials ("Ring Around the Collar," based on the singsong childhood taunt, usually wins the Most-Hated contests), but *getting noticed,* getting through the clutter of thousands of other ads, is a very important goal for most advertisers. Frequently, an obnoxious ad will be continued deliberately because it is still effectively selling the product to a large enough audience. Ideally, of course, an advertisement should be *both* noticed *and* liked. But, first things first.

Very few people *seek out* ads, except when consciously shopping for a particular product. Thus, at any one time, advertisers often face a market which is generally uninterested in their product. If consumers complain sometimes that there's too much advertising, advertisers also complain that there are too few people listening to their particular message. The marketplace of the mass media is quite like the din of the old time marketplace or the noisy oriental bazaar with sellers trying to shout or scream louder than their competitors. In such a situation, attention-getting is one of the main concerns of sellers and advertisers; however, there are so many variables that few advertisers even agree on a definition of what is meant by an attention-getter.

Attention-getting, here, is sorted into three main categories which cover most (if not all) of the techniques and devices usually mentioned: (1) **Physical attention-getters:** simple signals to our senses, usually sight and hearing; (2) **Emotional attention-getters:** words and images with strong emotional associations; (3) **Cognitive attention-getters:** certain patterns, appealing to our intellect, which lead us in, curious to find out more.

All three of these categories involve a focusing, or selective narrowing, of our thought and consciousness. All three aspects often co-exist and are inter-related. Most effective ads have many things going at once. multiple and simultaneous appeals. In order to understand ads better, we have to take them apart in smaller bits.

In analyzing any ad, remember that the typical 30-second spot television commercial is the *synthesis,* the end result, of months of work by a skilled team of people putting it together: writers, artists, designers, camera crews, a whole host of technicians and specialists, and often, market researchers, behavioral psychologists, advisors, and consultants. Thus, much has gone into the making of an ad, and much could be said about any ad. One way to start analyzing an ad is to look at the openers, the attention-getters.

(1) Physical attention-getters. The first major category refers to the simple perception of signals, the basic incoming stimuli received by our senses. Our sense of vision, for example, responds to shapes, sizes, colors, lights, and motion; our hearing responds to the intensity, frequency, and duration of sounds; we note their regularity, context and backgrounds. We notice the unusual, the atypical in our environment, as if an animal were suddenly alerted by a sound or a sight. Often we observe it until we're able to understand it, mentally deciding where to fit it into the rest of our experience. *Anything* which creates an unusual, atypical experience for our senses can be considered an attention-getter.

Attention-Getting

Simple visual and audio signals attracting our attention may be such things as a hand signal, waving at us or beckoning to us, accompanied by a smile or a come-hither look. Some attention-getting devices have been with us longer than others: the voices of merchants hawking their wares in the marketplace and circus barkers ("Hurry, Hurry, Hurry, Step Right Up...") have had a long history, as well as certain music associated with attention-getting: drum rolls, trumpet fanfares, and a whole range of attention calls made from brass bugles, ram's horns, and conch shells. Such elementary human signals to gain our attention are still very much with us, but modern advertising is not restricted to the yelling or shouting range of one human being.

In our Age of Hype (and Super-Hype), we often see so many intense things (flashing lights, loud noises, bright colors) that they tend to be the norm and lose their individual power of attention-getting. But, in a wider context, such Super-Hype may still retain its *collective* power of attention-getting: a person may not be able to distinguish among the various gaudy signs on a tourist strip (such as Las Vegas, Miami Beach, or Gatlinberg), but these areas can certainly be distinguished from their duller neighbors.

On television, attention-getters might include various electronic or photographic techniques as slow-motion replays, stop-action ("freeze frame"), time-lapse photography, split-screen pictures, close-ups, blurred focus, cross-sections, enlarged details, computer graphics, and so on. In print, attention-getters might include the various styles and designs in the typeface, graphics, photos, even Scratch-and-Sniff (encapsulated bubbles in the ink) novelties. In any large city, one is likely to see a dozen different attention-getters such as flags fluttering on used-car lots, billboard "sandwich men," flashing neon signs, loudspeakers, airplanes towing banners, blimps, hot air balloons, and searchlights at night.

Thus, in one way, we can talk about such simple things as lights, colors, noises, and moving objects as being attention-getters. But, there are other ways to gain our attention.

Very simply, we're *social beings,* accustomed to two-way conversations, the give and take of ordinary life. Someone looks at us, we look back at them. They talk to us, we listen. Someone points a finger at something, we look. Someone tells us to do something, we do it. Not always. Not all people. But enough, that such blunt attention-getting and "hard sells" *do* work with *some* people.

(2) Emotional attention-getters. The second major category refers to the use of any words or images (or sounds or smells) which have strong emotional associations. The use of the association technique is extremely common in all persuasion, not only as the initial attention-getter, but also as one of the main elements throughout the whole process of persuasion.

The association technique basically links three elements together: (1) the idea or product, with (2) something *already held favorably by, or desired by,* (3) the intended audience. (In "attack propaganda," the pattern is the same, but the middle element is reversed: linking the product or idea with something *already disliked or feared by* the intended audience.)

In one way, this is the easiest attention-getter to recognize: if you watch TV commercials or look at print ads, you'll be able to spot many emotional attention-getters used frequently in advertising: pretty girls, babies and cute kids, cats and dogs, nature scenery, scenes of playful "good times" with friends and family, smiling young lovers, churches and steeples, fluttering flags waving, and patriotic scenes.

Millions of combinations of such good things are possible. Later chapters will present some 24 common categories, together with lists of words and images often used. It's not necessary for you to know or to memorize all of these various categories, just as long as you recognize that the general pattern of this association technique is basically an appeal to our emotions.

Many critics of advertising *disapprove* of any emotional appeal and say that advertisers *shouldn't* do such things.

But here, the assumption is that the emotional appeal is one of the ways in which people have always used in trying to persuade others. The purpose here is not to condemn or to praise it, but to explain it.

Emotional appeals, made through the use of the association techniques, are very effective in getting our attention and in persuading us to action.

(3) Cognitive attention-getters. The third major category refers to anything of interest to our intellect. Just as we respond to certain emotional appeals, so also we respond to certain rational appeals to our thinking processes.

Here, we are concerned with those attention-getting devices which have certain patterns, appealing to our intellect, which lead us into a message, curious to find out more.

Most people are rather orderly processors of information, more or less following certain sorting patterns and certain sequences of ideas. Even if the current advertising blitz did not exist, people would still have a certain basic curiosity, interested about the world around them. Even without external encouragement, people would seek news and advice, exchange stories and information.

People are *information-seekers* and *benefit-seekers.* We seek information as a means to the end of seeking benefits. Advertisers, and other persuaders, are *information-providers* and *benefit-promisers.*

Here's a list of 10 common ways in which ads can get our attention by providing information or promising a benefit:

1. News
2. Lists & Displays
3. Claims & Promises
4. Advice
5. Lead-Ins
6. Questions
7. Stories
8. Demonstrations
9. Breaking Rules
10. Humor

1. **News.** People seek news. Many advertisements are basically *announcements* providing information about *new products, new uses* for existing products, or the *availability* of a product at a certain place or a certain price. Consider the thousands of new products invented, developed, and marketed in the past half-century. Automobiles, radio, television, hi-fi, home appliances, computers, calculators — all had to be introduced with some very basic explanations of *what* they were intended to do, and *how* they were to be used.

   Many local retail ads are simple announcements: the items are available, here and now, at this price. In early American newspapers, advertising began with such simple announcements: "a ship has landed in port, with these goods." Some critics would like to restrict advertising to this kind of basic information. But most ads today seek not only to inform, but also to persuade. In discussions of advertising, informational ads are generally the *least controversial;* usually the only criteria applied would be the truth or accuracy (or any significant omission) of the information.

2. **Lists & Displays.** People like to read lists, especially those which are rank-ordered such as "Top Ten Best Sellers," "5 Best Buys," "6 Easy Ways to Save Money," "8 Important Things to do before Christmas." The best-selling *Book of Lists,* a pot pourri of all kinds of lists, dramatically demonstrated our human love of lists, but nearly every newspaper and magazine uses listings as standard items. Advertisers, too, utilize our natural list-making and list-reading tendencies in the large number of ads which provide lists and rankings.

In addition, people like to look at displays of many items. We like to see selections, assortments, and varieties of products. Mail order catalogues, for example, are extremely popular; many people spend hours browsing through these displays of merchandise, just to see what's available, what are the prices and styles. Even when we can't buy something, we like to look at such displays: the reprints of the old Sears catalogues from the 1890s have become favorite nostalgia items. People are classifiers and collectors, delighting in making and seeing displays of many items. Variety *is* the spice of life. Advertisers attract our attention by offering us such displays: note how many ads show a selection of many varieties such as 20 different models of cars, 15 different dresses, 57 varieties of foods, or 10 different models of homes. Some of the key *verbs* in advertising are *"select"* and *"choose,"* sure indicators that an ad is dealing with lists or displays.

3. **Claims and Promises.** People are interested in claims and promises. A *claim,* as the term is used here, is a proposition or an assertion that a product *is* something, or *has* some quality, or *does* something. A *promise,* as the term is used here, means that it will *benefit* the buyer. Such claims and promises can be used as attention-getters, as well as during the whole process of persuasion.

The famous adman John Caples once recommended to advertising writers: "First and foremost, try to get self-interest into every headline you write. Make your headline suggest to the reader that here is something he wants."

Claims and promises *about the product itself* are discussed in this book (pp. 49-74) under a dozen general categories: *Superiority, Quantity, Efficiency, Beauty, Scarcity, Utility, Novelty, Stability, Reliability, Safety, Simplicity,* and *Rapidity.*

The specific words used will vary in different ads, but there are certain key words in many of these categories which are proven attention-getters, such as *free, exciting, new, quick and easy,* and *take advantage of.*

However, the *"added values"* — the emotional associations *suggested* by many ads are *not* intrinsic to the product, nor are they often *explicitly* claimed or promised. Two dozen categories of such "added values" relating to human needs and wants (such as *food, activity, health, sex, intimacy, belonging, esteem,* and *creativity*) are discussed more fully later (p. 75-130). In practice, many explicit claims and implicit suggestions cluster together, appear simultaneously, and are used both for attention-getters and the main body of the ad.

4. **Advice.** People often seek advice from others, especially from those with knowledge or authority. Many people look for certitude, for approval and permissions from outside sources. Even those people who would reject, or rebel against, *orders*

imposed by someone else, would welcome "advice" if it is given properly, that is, given as a *hint* or a *suggestion*.

The words *"how to..."* are some of the *most often used, most effective* words in advertising.

How-to-do-it books, on practically any subject, are the most frequently demanded books in libraries and bookstores. How-to-do-it articles are the staple features of popular magazines, such as the *Reader's Digest,* and tabloid newspapers such as the *National Inquirer.* One of the best attention-getters in practically any situation are these two simple words: *how to...*

5. **Lead-Ins.** People can be led into an idea by certain patterns within our language. There are a variety of ways in which we wait, in a kind of suspense, for the *completion* of an idea: the *resolution,* the *conclusion,* the *closure.* A question is the most commonly used and most obvious lead-in (See #6); logically, it's designed to elicit some kind of response. But a question is not the only opener which can be used as a "hook" or a "grabber." There are both obvious and subtle ways to arouse our interest.

Obvious ways would be the use of some kind of a teaser, a deliberate fragment, a conversation interrupted, a peek, a come-on for the "strip-tease effect." Movies, for example, often advertise "coming attractions" with film-clips of increasing tensions or exciting actions just about to climax. Such "cliff-hangers" are designed to leave us in suspense and bring us, as paying customers, to see the conclusion.

Using a *paradox,* a seemingly self-contradictory statement, is another obvious lead-in. Poets and preachers have often caught our attention by opening with paradoxical phrasings, and then explaining away the seeming contradictions. Advertisers too will catch our interest by telling us that here's the "fastest slow ride in town" or here's the "most complicated simple machine ever made."

Wanted! This one simple word, especially as a bold headline, is a very common, very effective attention-getter. Used as a lead-in, we read on, curious to find out *what* or *who* is wanted.

Other obvious lead-ins are the congratulatory praises and promises often seen as openers in direct mail advertisements: "Congratulations... You've been chosen... You've won... You've been selected... A free gift awaits you..."

More subtle lead-ins would include the use of sentence structures such as the *periodic sentence,* in which the full meaning is withheld until the end. Writers can pile up the front of a sentence with modifiers and dependent clauses, and withhold the basic subject-predicate relationship. Writers can stress *premise indicators* (Since, Because, etc.) which will logically lead to *conclusion indicators* (Thus, Therefore, etc.) at the end of the sentence or paragraph. Or, sentences can by hypotheticals *(If...*

then) which force us on to the ending: "If you're thinking of buying; If you like _____, you'll love _____ ; If you want _____ ; If you need _____ ."

6. **Questions.** Questions are the most obvious and explicit of any lead-in; they are very common and very important as attention-getters in advertising copy. In most cases, they are *rhetorical* questions, which *do not* expect an audible answer, but *are* seeking some kind of *inner response.* Pay attention to these questions very commonly asked in ads: *Why? Which? How? Who? Who else? Where else? Do you? Can you? When have you? Have you ever? Will you? When are you? Why not? Why pay more?*

In person-to-person selling, there are certain questions used as standard formalities. Usually, sales clerks are trained to ask polite questions which are designed both to be pleasant "openers" and to elicit a response. If such phrases are *not* used, some people are offended by the rudeness or curtness; if such formalities are *misused* and *overused,* then they seem to be phony, artificial, or obsequious. Consider the following attention-getters which you have heard frequently in personal selling, and think of how the tone of voice or facial expression accompanying these questions influenced your response:

> "May I help you?"
> "Is there anything I can show you?"
> "Do you have any questions?"
> "Have you seen our new item?"
> "Are you looking for a gift?"
> "Would you like a sample?"
> "Would you like to see something special?"
> "Is there something I can do?"
> "Have you heard about this?"

7. **Stories.** People are interested in stories, in narratives and dramatizations which involve people, their conflicts, and how they resolve them. TV commercials often use a story line as the form in which the product message is delivered, but such narratives are also common in print ads, cartoon strips, photo sequences, and even in one dramatic picture in which the rest of the story can be inferred.

The characters involved in these stories are usually presented as *role models,* setting examples of behavior, showing us how to act or respond in certain situations (usually by buying the product). Basically, such characters and stories can be divided into realistic and non-realistic presentations.

Realistic ("slice of life") stories used in advertising usually show close-to-life experiences of their intended audiences: situations such as dressing, shopping, eating, greetings and farewells, driving, doing household chores — washing, cooking, diapering, and so on. Usually "plain folks" actors are used in TV commercials to help create a stronger audience *empathy,* or strong identification, with such people "just like us." Conflicts are often common minor problems (headaches, dirty clothes) which can be resolved quickly with the product offered: a mild version of the "scare-and-sell" technique.

Non-realistic stories are often wish-fulfillment fantasies. In advertising, these are often commercial versions of our daydreams, our wishes and hopes, our aspirations acted out. The characters and situations are usually romanticized, idealized, exaggerated. The models used, for example, are likely to be the "beautiful people" doing very exciting or fashionable things (racing cars or yachts, going to elegant parties in rich homes, and walking on white sandy beaches), then using the product (beer, cola, clothes, or cosmetics).

Borderlines will exist between reality and fantasy, varying with the audience's response. A street-interview scene, for example, may be realistic to some; to others it might involve their fantasy dream of *esteem:* somebody asking *their opinion* about something. Yet the general areas of realistic and non-realistic stories are recognizable, even though there will be an occasional attention-getting *variation:* such as inserting a non-realistic element into a realistic scene (e.g., a typical household scene in which a medieval knight suddenly appears, holding a box of soap).

Parodies ("take-offs") are attention-getters. Some ads follow the same basic storyline patterns (stock situations and visual cliches) previously established in noncommercial narratives: western stories, police adventure stories, science-fiction, song-and-dance musicals ("production numbers"). Audiences often recognize the familiar patterns, then notice the differences in the commercial version; the intent and the result are frequently humorous.

In addition to the use of stories as attention-getters *within* an advertisement, consider the broader picture that stories, *unrelated to any specific ad,* are often used as part of the entertainments which lure us to the places where the ads will be on television, in newspapers and magazines.

Although the public may envision the role of television as *providing entertainment to the public,* most television executives see their business as *delivering audiences to their advertisers.* The function of the entertaining stories, the programs, is to attract an audience in one place where they can see and hear "the pitch."

The close similarity between modern television programming and the oldfashioned "medicine show" selling "snake oil" and other fraudulent remedies can be seen in this description found in

James Young's *The Toadstool Millionaires,* a fascinating history of patent medicines in the nineteenth century:

> Whatever medicine was sold, and whatever attractions were used to lure the citizenry, the sales pitch was always sandwiched in between entertainment. It would not do to begin selling at once, for the audience would feel themselves short-changed. A proper mood needed creating. This mood was not one thing. It might be awe at expert marksmanship. It might be delight at black-face comedy. It might be the slightly naughty shock of seeing a magician pull lingerie from grandpa's pocket. The mood was something that beguiled a crowd, drove from their minds extraneous concerns, and focused attention upon a novel and entrancing spectacle. Thus they were made receptive. Even with such a build-up, no medicine man was cocky enough to count on holding his audience during the sales pitch without the promise of more free entertainment to come. The after-piece was a fixed part of every show.
>
> When the pitchman took over, he did not begin by mentioning medicine... Any talk of medicine and money was gradually and gingerly approached.

8. **Demonstrations.** People are interested in demonstrations which explain and illustrate by showing how something works or how it's used. Demonstrations are very strong forms of *proof*. It's much more effective *to show* something working than simply *to say* that it can work. Demonstrations, in all their various forms (including free samples and "hands-on" test-drives) lend credibility and confidence to any persuasion attempt. Because it is such an effective technique, many persuaders will use demonstrations. People are more likely to believe in *demonstrations* than in verbal *claims* and *promises*.

This has always created some problems relating to *deceptive* demonstrations. In the past, for example, some demonstrations could be faked: worthless mines could be "salted" with gold, horses "doctored" to look better, livestock "watered" to add weight. But today the *potential* for wholesale deception is far greater. On television, for example, there are so many ways of creating *illusions,* with visuals and special effects, that a demonstration can be easily altered. Thus the Federal Trade Commission (FTC) has probably given more attention to the problems of demonstrations than to any other form of deceptive advertising.

Four common kinds of demonstrations are: *step-by-step* demonstrations showing the process or sequence of how something works, often used to introduce new products or complicated ones; *before-and-after* demonstrations showing the effects, results or the consequences, often used with *"efficiency"* claims; *side-by-side* comparison demonstrations, often used with *"superiority"* and *"quantity"* claims demonstrating that one product "is better" or "has more" than others; *behind-the-scenes* demonstrations, (or "inside story" or "backstage") showing how something was made, or who made it or the reasons behind it, often used to justify expense or to humanize a corporation.

9. **Breaking Rules.** People notice when rules are broken, that is, when *deviations* are made from any standard or customary procedure. Such deviation is inversely related to repetition techniques because any departure from the norm implies that the standard convention had been previously established by long-term repetition within the culture. Unconventional behavior may be annoying, but it is attention-getting.

Common deviations used by advertisers as attention-getters include deliberate misspellings (Kathy's Kwicky Kitchen, Su-Z-Q's, Kof-E-Brake), deliberate use of "bad grammar" ("Us Taryton smokers would rather fight than switch"), upside-down billboard signs, and so on. Mild oaths ("hell" and "damn") are sometimes used as attention-getters in ads; stronger vulgarity is rarely used in commercial advertising, but frequently in political attack language.

10. **Humor.** Often used as an attention-getter, humor also involves some kind of deviation from the norm. Most definitions of humor point out that it relates to something which is unexpected, unanticipated, inappropriate, or incongruous to the situation. We laugh at many things simply because they do not make sense logically, they do not follow, or they do not belong.

The humor usually seen in advertising is more likely to be the mild, mellow lighthearted humor which provokes a smile or a chuckle rather than a full laugh. In ads, we're likely to *laugh with,* rather than *laugh at,* the speaker. The biting humor of satire is seldom found in ads, more frequently in political attacks.

Self-depreciating humor is sometimes used in ads; but this is usually a form of the *concessive argument.* Volkswagon, for example, might kid their own cars as being "plain" or "ugly" (concede a minor point) because their major selling points are "superiority," "economy," "efficiency," and "practicality."

Humor as an attention-getter, can take many forms ranging from pie-throwing *slapstick* and *sight gags* to the witty cleverness of *puns.* Word play is very common in advertising; puns abound in headlines, copy, and even in the names of products and retail stores. Sexual puns, *double entendres,* are frequently used in some advertising contexts (men's magazines) as attention-getters.

To recap: attention-getting can refer to: (1) *Physical attention-getters* — the simple signals to our senses — lights, colors, sounds, motions; (2) *Emotional attention-getters* — words or images with strong emotional associations — such as pretty faces, pets, babies and cute kids, and natural scenery; (3) *Cognitive attention-getters* — a wide variety of things appealing to our intellect and curiosity, such as news, lists, displays, advice, and stories. Anytime our attention has been focused on *one* ad, or anytime we can remember the brand name, corporation name, logo or signature, of any item, among the hundreds of thousands of competing ads, then the attention-getters have been effective. Ultimately, an effective ad has to get response, but *first* it has to get attention.

PHYSICAL ATTENTION-GETTERS

Any atypical, unusual, abnormal, irregular, odd, unexpected...

motion
sights
  shapes
  sizes
  colors
  lights
  backgrounds
sounds
  intensity
  tone
  pattern
including, such things as:
— typeface
— graphics
— close-ups
— time-lapse
— split-screen
— freeze-frame
— slow-motion
— computer graphics
— electronic sounds

EMOTIONAL ATTENTION-GETTERS

Related to our memory and emotional associations.

Some *common* subjects:

— pretty girls
— babies & cute kids
— cats & dogs
— friends & family
— "good times"

For a fuller listing of 24 major categories of such hopes and dreams (and the opposing fears and nightmares used in "scare-and-sell" techniques), see pp. 75-130.

COGNITIVE ATTENTION-GETTERS

Related to our cognitive processes of thought.

1. News!
2. Lists & Displays
3. Claims & Promises
4. Advice (How to...)
5. Lead-Ins
6. Questions
7. Stories
8. Demonstrations
9. Breaking Rules
10. Humor

2

CONFIDENCE-BUILDING

Everyone gets information from other people. We often believe a message simply on the basis of our belief in, or liking of, the speaker. If we already like the speaker, it's likely we'll like what the speaker says.

Establishing trust is basic. All persuaders ("good" or "bad," public or private) can be analyzed in terms of what "image" they project. We believe in, and we buy from, people we trust. Aristotle, over two thousand years ago, claimed that the most effective way to persuade was to project the image *(ethos)* of being:
1) **expert,** that is, knowledgeable, informed, competent, wise, prudent, a person of good judgment and good sense; and
2) **sincere,** that is, honest, trustworthy, truthful, open, candid, a person of integrity and good moral character;
3) **benevolent,** that is, friendly to the audience, a friend, an ally, a benefactor, a person of good will, with your interest in mind: "on *your* side."

It would be nice if these qualities were really genuine, but Aristotle points out that it's still *very effective* for the persuader even if there is only the *appearance* of these qualities of expertise, sincerity, and benevolence. One of the major concerns about modern advertising is the exploitation of these techniques of image-building.

In the past, the study of rhetoric focused on the *individual* as a persuader, often discussing how the individual can present the best image. Today, the presentation of "self" is often a *corporate* process as committees within large corporations select the kind of people to be used to present or to endorse their products.

Governments and their functionaries, corporations and their products, are always begging for our trust, our belief, our confidence in them. "Trust me" is the standard pitch of practically every politician and every product peddled.

Who, then, can be trusted? Reach in your pocket. Look at the coins or the bills. The official motto of this country is "In God We Trust." And the unofficial ending, hallowed in American folklore, and found in restaurants and bars and stores from coast to coast, is that bit of folk wisdom which says, "All others pay cash!"

Such a folksy realistic attitude might be called a healthy skepticism. Certainly one of the most important survival skills which parents, teachers, and schools can encourage today is an attitude of healthy skepticism, a moderate position avoiding the extremes of believing everything or believing nothing.

Most people, in their daily person-to-person communications with others do avoid the extremes; they know that different people can be trusted, or not trusted, in varying degrees. By experience, we gradually make these judgments about our friends and acquaintances. Yet some people have a tendency to take an all-or-nothing position when dealing with corporate communications, with those constant messages and ads being sent out to us by governments and corporations. But, here too, we need a healthy skepticism. We must avoid being either fools or cynics. We cannot survive if we believe everything, nor if we believe nothing.

Foremost among our modern survival skills, in a corporate society with such sophisticated persuasion techniques, must be the ability to analyze language and to make critical judgments, to transform vague trust or distrust into specific acceptance or rejection, and to evaluate those who seek our trust and confidence.

If a democratic society is to remain free, citizens should not be encouraged to be docile, gullible, or naive. One of the purposes of this book is to take away some of the *illusions* about persuasion techniques and to replace them with realistic information, practical attitudes, and approaches to cope with language manipulation by the powerful persuaders in our society. In person-to-person communication, we learn *degrees of trust*. We need to apply this same kind of awareness

Confidence-Building

to the corporate persuaders. One of the best ways to make reasonable decisions as to what degree of trust we place in a speaker is to learn the techniques used by modern professional persuaders.

As citizens and consumers, for example, we can become more aware of (1) the overall strategy of image-building of projecting a good image in terms of *expertise, sincerity,* and *benevolence;* (2) the specific words and images commonly used; (3) the role of *presenters* (speakers, endorsers, testimonials) and brand names; and (4) the various "personal touch" devices of modern mass communications.

The basic strategy of establishing an *ethos,* or building confidence, is to put the audience in a good mood, trusting and receptive, toward the speaker before the main part of "the pitch" begins. Sometimes this may take place *within* a single ad or message; an unknown speaker, for example, usually has this problem of establishing an image. However, in much advertising today, image-building often takes place in a *wider context:* frequently, we already know or like the speaker and the brand name. A great deal of long-term conditioning propaganda (various forms of "public relations," "corporate advertising," and goodwill gestures, discussed later) usually occurs within a society, functioning as a solid base on which to build any specific ad campaign.

Flattery is a common tactic to put an audience in a good mood. Persuaders often appeal to our pride and vanity. If flattery is done well, we'll never notice it. If it is overdone and obvious to us, we're apt to be suspicious. But, even then, flattery has a persuasive way of convincing us that perhaps we *do* deserve the praise directed our way. To intensify the "good" of the audience — the "good" they really are, or the "good" they'd like to be — is a sure way for the persuader to become welcome.

The best persuasion is *smooth,* is that which goes *unnoticed,* is that which soothes, lulls, relaxes, creates trust, seems natural, credible, believable, and is non-threatening. Later, if a transaction proves unsatisfactory, we might complain that we were seduced, or set up, or talked into it by a smooth talker. But, note the emphasis we usually place on the smoothness of effective persuasion.

Words can be used to help build a good image. Often we see persuaders simply asserting that they are competent, trustworthy, and on our side. Listed here are some common phrasings used as "Confidence" words emphasizing trust in the *speaker* or *seller;* later in the book, a closely-related term "Reliability" is used to categorize claims emphasizing good qualities inherent in the *product.*

Just as *"the pitch"* (Hi!/Trust Me/ You Need/ Hurry/Buy) is a useful way to emphasize the *form,* the sequential pattern, of persuasion, so also here's a useful formula sentence to focus on the *content* of the persuader's words in such image-building, in establishing an ethos: **"I am competent and trustworthy; from me, you'll get..."***

The specific *wording* can very; many surface variations are possible. The specific *emphasis* can vary: "authority figures" may stress expertise, "friend figures" may stress kindness. There's even some leeway and variation in how people *define* and *sub-categorize* these concepts, in relation to different contexts and situations. But, basically, there are three major concepts (expertise, sincerity, benevolence) involved when persuaders say "Trust Me."

Nonverbal ways of suggesting trustworthiness have always been very important in inter-personal dealings as we display and recognize so many subtle cues as we talk to each other. But, the importance of nonverbals, and of understanding such body language, has grown enormously since the advent of television. Visual images and other nonverbal signals now have an even greater role to play in the basic "confidence" appeal.

On television, for example, speakers will frequently talk to us, stressing the warmth of the second person pronoun "you" as the camera zooms close-up on their eyes looking directly at us. Well trained in the appropriate body language, these presenters are likely to give us the slight smile or the sincere look, the gestures with the open hand upheld, the direct eye contact, the voice tone helping to create the appropriate mood or atmosphere. Sometimes it's the relaxed, informality of a friendly conversation; sometimes it's the tone of the fatherly advice or motherly concern. But whatever mood, there's a lot of effort going into such studied casualness.

---

*[In an earlier work *(English Journal,* December, 1980) analyzing election rhetoric, I've recommended a single sentence summing up the basic claims and promises of politicians: *"I am competent and trustworthy; from me, you'll get more (good) and less (bad)."* Note that the first part of this sentence epitomizes the basic claims of all persuaders; in the latter part, the comparative factor (more/less) in the promises stresses the competitive nature of an election. That article provides operational definitions, subcategories and the related contradictories of those three key concepts in a political context.]

CONFIDENCE-BUILDING

absolutely safe
assure, assurance, rest assured
candid, candor
certain, certainly
concern, concerned
confident, confidence
depend, dependable
established
experience, experienced
expert, expertise
fair
friend, friendly, friendship
guarantee, guaranty
honest, honesty
informed
integrity
interest, interested
kind, kindly
knowledgeable
no obligation
no risk
nothing to lose
on *your* side
one of us
positive, positively
proven
prudent
reasonable
recommended
rely, reliable
reputable, reputation
responsible
satisfaction guaranteed
sincere, sincerity
straight, straightforward
trust, trustworthy
true, truth, truthful
wise, wisdom

These nonchalant smiles, sincere looks, and sympathetic headnods can be rehearsed and practiced, taped and re-taped, edited, tested, and re-edited, until the final televised version presents the perfect result designed to please the largest number of people. Thus, modern advertising gives great attention to the "presenters," those people selected to deliver the messages: the models, actors, and celebrities who appear in ads on television and in photographs, and even the mellow voices who do the voice-overs. More recently, political strategists are adapting these tactics, making sure that their candidates have such convincing appearances in their TV commercials.

Presenters, in relation to the idea of a *projected image,* can be divided into two basic categories: *authority figures* and *friend figures.*

Authority figures are those presenters whom we trust or like because they suggest the good aspects of the nurturing parent: the protective care, wisdom, and guidance of the kind father or mother, or of parent surrogates, such as teachers, advisors, leaders, mentors, or ministers. The emphasis here is on expertise, knowledge, competency, and certitude.

Friend figures are those presenters whom we trust or like because they suggest people we would *like to be,* or *to be with,* or *be liked by;* these friends can range from "plain folks" to idealized "beautiful people" of our wish-fulfillment dreams, or even "cute" fictional characters or animals.

Presenters, in the broadest sense, are the persons who deliver the messages in ads. Basically they say *"Buy* this"; they need not endorse or explicitly say *"I like* this" or *"I use* this," but usually such an endorsement is implied. In "scare-and-sell" ads, usually the problem is dramatized, then an authority figure or a friend figure suggests the solution.

Endorsements (or testimonials) are specific statements of recommendation or approval in which the speaker *explicitly* says "I like this" or "I use this." Politics as well as advertising makes extensive use of testimonials, relying on the transferring of a favorable aura or overtones from one person to another.

Most advertisers do *not* expect many people to make *conscious* decisions based on such testimonials. While there may be *some* people extremely insecure, dependent, naive, or gullible, *not many* people would consciously rush out to buy Superbread because their heroes endorse it. But, we do *subconsciously* imitate, or model after, other people we like or admire. Some of our behavior models are from our first-hand experience: parents, teachers, and friends.

Other behavior models are known to us from vicarious, second-hand experience: those people we read about, or see on television — movie stars, fashion models, athletes, social and political leaders.

Every era has its beautiful people, admired and envied by millions. Often, such people can be rented by corporations who know that pretty faces can sell products. Sometimes this is literally true: *beautiful women* are the most commonly-used presenters in magazine advertisements and television commercials. But, there are many variations possible: for example, male sports heroes are used for some products, business executives for others, and, for others, even fictional characters.

Fictional characters, both human and animal, can be created to present a product. Often cheaper and much easier to control than real celebrities, such *"continuing central characters"* (advertising jargon) — or *"plastic people"* (teenage slang) — can be planned for their usefulness in both television and print advertising. Well known characters include: Ronald McDonald, Betty Crocker, Aunt Jemima, Buster Brown, Madge the Manicurist, Morris the Cat, Charlie Tuna, the Pillsbury Doughboy, the Marlboro Man, the Morton Salt Girl, the Jolly Green Giant, and Speedy Alka-Seltzer. Most of these fictional characters could probably be described as being "cute," that is, likable or loveable, like a doll or a pet, a variation of the *"friend figure."*

Variations on basic themes are common. Some modeling agencies, for example, specialize in providing models who look like famous celebrities. Often the intent is not so much to save money by hiring a substitute as it is to be an attention-getting device because audiences often delight in seeing a good imitation. Other modeling agencies specialize in providing "uglies" or "plain folks" for certain commercials which are designed to avoid the "slick" look associated with beautiful models. Large corporations, for example, often seek to humanize their image, to make it more credible or trusty, by using such "plain folks" techniques.

Deception and misrepresentation are possible, not only in the explicit statements made by presenters, but also in the implied suggestions made by their appearance linking them with the product. Over the years, the FTC has tried to prevent deceptive advertising by setting up guidelines defining the kinds of testimonials and endorsements which are honest and fair, and those which are deceptive and unfair. Since 1975, these guidelines have become more specific and many of the worst violations (such as, white-coated "doctors") no longer appear. Basically, the FTC encourages testimonials to be from experts, within the area of their expertise, to be honest and typical; the FTC frowns on distortion, quotes out of context, phony experts, the illusion of government approval, lies, and so on. Such guidelines have helped to remove *hard-core* deception, but borderline cases continually appear as some advertisers do try to get away with as much as they can.

Establishing trust, or building confidence, in a product or person need not be deceptive nor artificial. There are many honest people, many good products, and many mutual benefits shared between sellers and buyers.

Good craftsmen, for example, in the pre-industrial age, put their own marking on the pottery and silverware they made as a way of identifying their work. As such *trademarks,* and later *brand names,* became associated with reputable established companies and quality products, more and more sellers began to use trademarks and brand names as merchandising tools. Today, in the United States, there are nearly 500,000 registered trademarks, most of which are competing to be known and liked by the public.

Brand names are important confidence builders. Many corporations and advertisers spend a great deal of time and money to build a reputation for their products. "Brand loyalty" is the dream of every seller: that buyers would know, trust, and prefer their brand. In general, brand name products and established stores *are* more trustworthy than unbranded items and unknown stores.

In business today, a well known and trusted name is worth a lot of money. A reputable company often takes great effort in protecting its name, not only in its internal operations (such as, product quality-control, guarantees, customer relations) but also with external factors. Famous brands are often imitated, copied, pirated, and counterfeited. Alas, there are even disadvantages in gaining the confidence and trust of the public.

Mass communications uses various devices today to give the personal touch to persuasion messages directed at millions of people. Direct mail advertising, for example, has long used some very clever techniques to personalize mail: print typefaces giving "personal" letters the appearance of being hand-typed; signatures printed in another ink, or even made with handwriting machines, so that the letters appear to be personally signed. (U.S. Presidents use such machines so that their secretarial staff can produce thousands of artificial "personal letters" every day.) A very effective technique is the use of computers to personalize messages with *inserts* of the receiver's own name, address, locale, and so on. People who used to throw away the mail addressed to "Occupant" or "Homeowner," now are reading the computer written letters directed, personally, to them: "Dear Mr. Tom Jones, Is your house at 871 Oak Street adequately insured?"

Telephones are a favorite tool of modern sellers. A telephone call is a great attention-getter because very few people will let a phone keep ringing. Most people are curious or polite, and will often interrupt all other activity to answer the phone. But, if the caller is trying to sell us something, or if we recognize the smooth practiced sales pitch being delivered from some "boiler room" operation, in which dozens of phone solicitors are talking to potential customers, we may become annoyed.

In the past, there was always a human being, no matter how annoying, at the other end of the line: the telephone was a genuine *interpersonal* machine. However, new technology now makes it possible for a computer to "dial" the number, then activate a tape-recorded sales message when we answer the phone. These sophisticated devices are growing in popularity with advertisers (and with politicians during election campaigns), creating a controversy about the intrusion on our privacy by means of such "junk phone calls." Several states have already enacted some restrictions on their use, but there's no uniform national policy.

To recap: The most effective way to persuade is by gaining the trust of the audience by projecting the image of being *expert, sincere,* and *benevolent.* Persuaders seek this appearance, try to put us in a good mood toward them, often flatter us or soothe us. Confidence-building words and images (including nonverbal gestures, expressions, such as smiles and "sincere" voicetones) are used, especially by admired or trusted *presenters* (including "authority figures" and "friend figures"). Technical devices are used in the mass media to create the illusion of the "personal touch."

To Analyze an Ad, Ask these Key Questions:

- Do you *recognize, already know* (from earlier repetition) the *brand name* ? *company* ? *symbol* ? *package* ?

- Do you *already know, like,* and *trust* the *"presenters":* the endorsers, actors, models?

- Are these *"presenters"* **authority figures** (expert, wise, protective, caring)? Or, are they **friend figures** (someone you like, like to be, "on your side" — including "cute" cartoons, animals)?

- What key **words** are used? (Trust, Sincere, etc.) **Nonverbals?** (smiles, voice tones, sincere look).

- In **mail** ads, are computer-written "personalized" touches used? On **telephone:** tapes ? scripts ?

3

DESIRE-STIMULATING

After *getting attention* ("Hi!") and *establishing confidence* ("Trust Me"), the main part of "the pitch" intensifies *desire* by promising benefits: a pleasure to be gained, a pain to be avoided, a possession to be safeguarded, a problem to be solved. Advertisers often call *this reason why* people want something, the "main selling point." The body (the content, the substance) of most ads involves the *stimulating* and *focusing* of specific human needs and wants: *"You Need."*

This chapter will show how our *benefit-seeking* and the persuaders' *benefit-promising* are inter-related; it will sort out many of these possible benefits, and show how hundreds of words and images fit into these patterns. In addition, these word lists are cross-referenced to the rear of this book ("Reference Guide"), showing specifically how these are used by some forty kinds of products and services, (soft drinks, beer, cosmetics, cars, stereos, home repairs, airlines, etc.) representing thousands of brands today, and billions of dollars worth of advertising.

Old & New Views

The traditional view of advertising, still held by many people, stressed the concept of a "Maker" praising the product; an auto manufacturer, for example, might focus on the "economy" or "utility" of its products. Such a business concept was closely related to the "better mousetrap" idea that all a business had to do was to build a better product and the world would eagerly seek it out. Prior to World War II, most American advertising was thus, **product-oriented**. At best, it informed the public about the genuine merits of products; at worst, it made false and deceptive claims. But, most commonly, it was characterized by superlatives and self-praise: "puffery."

(This chapter lists and discusses twelve general categories of advertising claims covering nearly every conceivable thing which can be said about the **intrinsic merits** of a product: *Superiority, Quantity, Beauty, Efficiency, Scarcity, Novelty, Stability, Reliability, Simplicity, Utility, Rapidity,* and *Safety.*)

However, by the 1950's, a major shift developed as advertising became increasingly **audience-oriented,** that is, more focused on human desires, the needs and wants of the target audience. This view of advertising emphasizes the concept of the "Persuader" seeking the audience's response. The emphasis shifted away from a focus on the *intrinsic* merits of the product (product-as-hero ads) to a focus on the benefits desired by the buyer. Often, these benefits were the intangible "**added values**" — the status or prestige of a name brand, the promise of popularity or sex appeal, the various dreams and fantasies, hopes, and wishes of the audience.

(This chapter lists and discusses some two dozen categories of human needs and wants, covering nearly every kind of desire analyzed by various psychologists and philosophers: *food, health, sex, security, certitude, territory, belonging, esteem, play, curiosity, creativity, etc.*)

In practice, most ads are still a mixture of product-praise and audience-engagement. But, in degree, there has been a noticeable shift away from straight informational ads, and even "puffery" about a products, to ads with an emphasis on stimulating and focusing our desires.

Benefit-seeking

This book's basic premise is that *all people are benefit-seekers* and that *persuaders are benefit-promisers*. This important premise is not accepted by everyone (some people want to restrict advertising to information, denying its function as persuasion) and this premise is seldom stated so bluntly and explicitly. But, if we start here, we can see more clearly the transaction involved between our own benefit-seeking and the benefit-promising of persuaders.

To begin, we need to look at what we mean by a benefit, the definition of the "good." Traditionally, philosophers and moralists have struggled with such problems as trying to define the *"good,"* the *"good life," "happiness,"* and *"pleasure."* Today, psychologists (such as Maslow) are more likely to be concerned with the definition and classification of various "goods" in terms of human motivation, of human needs and wants. Thus, we have many different definitions and many different lists and categories of "goods" as developed by different observers. Not only are these terms *relative* (what's "good" for one person may be "bad" for another), but also ambiguous.

People think about them and talk about them in different ways. One person may talk about the "good life" in terms of *abstractions* ("To me, the good life is a life of *integrity, creative fulfillment,* seeking *beauty* and *harmony* with nature..."), another may speak in terms of *specific behaviors* ("To me, the good life is listening to records, riding my motorcycle, and surfing.")

Such ambiguities exist in our language. We can't change this, but in this book, we'll call attention to the problem by always using *quotes* or *parentheses* when using the words "good" and "bad" to suggest that *any* "good" or "bad," however conceived or defined by a person, can be inserted.

People are benefit-seekers: for survival and growth, we seek after the "good" — as we perceive it. There's so much common agreement to this generalization that it can be described as a "ho hum" truism: so what! But, once we accept this as a premise, there are certain implied relationships which follow. For example, for every "good" there's an opposite "bad" which is either the *contradictory or the absence* of the "good." So also, every "good" and "bad" can be described in terms of *degree:* very "good," very "bad," "so-so" are common ways of talking about the scale or range of degree. Or, consider that every "good" or "bad" condition has related *causes* and related *effects;* or that every "good" that we seek is related to our *behaviors* (what we do), our *beliefs* (what we think), and our *emotions* (how we feel). Or, consider that every such "good" and "bad" has a whole *cluster* of such relationships associated with it, and that the whole cluster can be triggered in our mind by any of the parts.

One relationship, useful for our purposes here, is to describe our *basic behaviors as benefit-seekers* in terms of two factors: (1) our perception of "good" and "bad"; and (2) our posession — that is, whether we *have* it, or *do not have* it.

Thus, the dynamics of our benefit-seeking can be described in terms of four basic behaviors: if people *have* a "good," they want to *keep* it (protection); if people have a "bad," they want to *change* it (relief); if people *don't have* a "good," they want to *get* it (acquisition); if people *don't have* a "bad" they want to *avoid* it (prevention). Most, if not all, persuasion can be related to these four kinds of benefit-seeking behaviors.

	"good"	"bad"
"have"	KEEP THE "GOOD"	CHANGE THE "BAD"
"have not"	GET THE "GOOD"	AVOID THE "BAD"

(Figure 1)

Illustrating this with a four-part grid (Figure 1) calls attention to four different aspects of our benefit-seeking. All aspects exist simultaneously, but usually one is emphasized or *explicitly stated* while the others are *implicitly suggested*. For example, most ads simply say GET a *"good,"* but this simultaneously implies AVOID the "bad" or CHANGE the "bad." Sometimes ads explicitly say *"buy* this and *save* money" (that is, GET a "good" and KEEP a "good"). This double-barreled approach is a seeming paradox which urges us to save money by spending it. Yet this tandem coupling of these two aspects is very common and is usually explainable by the qualifications made: e.g., "you'll save money *in the long run* by buying this now."

Observers need not try to pigeonhole an ad into one category, or use this grid as an inflexible straightjacket in analyzing persuasion. But, frequently a *dominant impression* can be noted easily. The most important thing for us, as observers and analysts, is to recognize our own involvement in benefit-seeking and to get an overall sense of what to expect from persuaders.

We should also be able to recognize when we are *not involved,* when we are not seeking the particular benefits being offered. We often ignore, or even get irritated at, those ads not directed at us. If we don't have headaches or hemorrhoids, we may not be the target audience for the TV commercials on the nightly news; if we don't have pimples, we may not be interested in the promises of salvation offered on some of the radio stations.

Before we go on to examine the basic behaviors of *persuaders*, it's worth a closer look at each of the four parts of this grid illustrating our basic behaviors as *benefit-seekers. (Figure 2)*

KEEP THE "GOOD"	CHANGE THE "BAD"
KEY VERBS: Keep, Save, Protect, Defend, Maintain, Retain, Uphold Have, Own, Support, Hold, Invest, Safeguard	KEY VERBS: Change, Relieve, Reduce Stop, Cure, Expel, Eliminate, Eject, Escape, Reject, Discard, Fight, Struggle, Abandon, Oust, Destroy, Get Rid Of; RELATED: Renew, Restore, Reform, Revive, Repair.
FUNCTION: Protection	FUNCTION: Expulsion, Relief
IN POLITICS: "Establishment" Rhetoric (status quo)	IN POLITICS: Reform & Revolutionary Rhetoric
RELATED EMOTIONS: Satisfaction, Contentment, Joy	RELATED EMOTIONS: Anger, Frustration
GET THE "GOOD"	AVOID THE "BAD"
KEY VERBS: Get, Buy, Use, Try, Enjoy, Purchase, Obtain, Select, Choose; *Specific Behaviors,* e.g., Eat, Drink, Taste, Smoke, Drive, Wear, See, Listen To, Feel, Experience, Shop At, Go To, Come To, Stay At, Play With, Travel On.	KEY VERBS: Prevent, Avoid, Stop, Exclude, Resist, Check, Retard, Avert, Block, Prohibit, Forbid, Deny, Repell, Shut Out, Keep Out Of, Don't Let, Don't Allow
FUNCTION: Acquisition, Growth	FUNCTION: Prevention
IN POLITICS: Promises	IN POLITICS: Warnings
RELATION EMOTIONS: Desire, Envy, Anticipation	RELATED EMOTIONS: Fear, Anxiety

(Figure 2)

KEEP THE "GOOD." Some persuasion appeals to our desire for **protection,** to safeguard the "goods" which we already possess. In political persuasion, for example, this is the rhetoric of the "Haves," the Establishment defending the *status quo*. Many patriotic pleas (as well as many "causes") call for a defense of the "good" which the group possesses. Relatively fewer commercial advertisements stress this aspect, but those that do are the various products and services sold as a *means* to protect *something else we already possess:* home maintenance products, car-care products, soaps and cleansers, investment and savings programs stressing protection of existing assets, and so on. The key verbs commonly used here: *keep, save, protect, maintain, retain, uphold, have, own, support, hold,* etc.

GET THE "GOOD." Most commercial advertising, perhaps 80% or 90%, in an affluent society simply emphasizes **acquisition.** There are so many consumer goods, and our desires can be so unlimited, that advertisers simply try to persuade us that their particular product is a "good" deserving a high priority on our list. Although our desires may be unlimited, our money and our time are not. Growing up in a world of hype, of stimulated desires and promises of benefits can lead to many personal problems (conflicts, frustrations, fears, dissatisfactions) and to social problems. Poor people, for example, who cannot afford many items, are being exposed daily to the same intense persuasion targeted at a richer audience. Such stimulation of desire *implies* a purchase transaction — that we *buy* the goods, not shoplift or steal them! The key verbs commonly used: *buy, get, use, try, enjoy, purchase, obtain, select, choose;* and verbs appropriate to the use of specific products, such as: *eat, drink, taste, smoke, drive, wear, see, hear, listen to, feel, experience, shop at, go to, come to, stay at, play with, travel on,* etc.

CHANGE THE "BAD." Some persuasion appeals to our desire for **relief** if we have a "bad." In political persuasion, this is the rhetoric of reform and revolution. In commercial advertising, such appeals to change a "bad" make up a relatively small, but very sensitive area: people who are suffering pain, for example, are a very vulnerable audience. Throughout history, for example, frauds and quacks have sold "cures" to desperate people. Today, although FDA and FTC regulations have reduced fraudulent ad claims, hard-core frauds still steal millions from cancer victims. With legitimate over-the-counter drugs (e.g., headache remedies), borderline problems have always existed; at present, for example, FTC requires certain qualifying words ("aids . . . helps . . . may relieve . . . ") and restricts certain TV techniques (white-coated "doctors"). Many self-improvement plans (diets, health clubs, etc.) also stress the "bad" and promise to change it. The key verbs commonly used here: *change, relieve, reduce, stop, cure, expel, eliminate, eject, escape, reject, fight, struggle, abandon, oust, destroy, get rid of.*

Closely related is a variation which calls for *renewal* or *reform*. Although revolutionary rhetoric may *categorically* condemn the status quo, reform rhetoric *qualifies* by using terms *(renew, restore, reform, revive, repair,* etc.) which imply that a *basic* "good" exists, and has been only *temporarily* or *partially* lost because of the opposition. So also the religious rhetoric of renewal: "born again," "rebirth," "new beginning," "fresh start," "starting over," etc.

AVOID THE "BAD." Some persuasion relates to our desire for **prevention** against a "bad." Here, the term **"scare-and-sell"** is a useful label to describe any ad which emphasizes fear of a potential "bad." Instead of peddling hopes and dreams, this approach emphasizes fear and nightmares. Intensifying the seriousness of a threat is common in all political persuasion, religious rhetoric, and "cause" propaganda. We know, for example, that a sure sign of a Pentagon budget request is the flood of preparatory press releases pointing with alarm at growing Soviet strength. Whether saving souls from hellfire, or saving seals from extinction, persuaders know that the greater the threat is intensified, the greater is the need for their remedy. Fear is a powerful human emotion in itself and persuaders can always claim that they give such *warnings* for "your own benefit" and if we don't heed their advice... ("Well, I *told* you so..."). Some consumer ads use this approach of warning about a problem, then offering a solution. For example, safety items (e.g., tires, batteries, smoke alarms, fire insurance, traveler's checks) often dramatize horrible tragedies which can be avoided by the precaution of buying the product. So also, some cosmetics (e.g., mouthwash, deodorants) play on our fears of social tragedies: "You'll be unloved, unwanted, rejected... unless you buy our product...".

If such "scare-and-sell" appeals in advertising are *not credible* or *too intense,* people may complain about them. But, the problem/solution pattern is quite commonly used and effective in many ads. In the accompanying word lists, brief "scare-and-sell" lists will appear for *every* category to point out that this tactic *could be* used in *any* situation. Key verbs commonly used here: *prevent, avoid, stop, exclude, resist, retard, block, prohibit, deny, shut out, keep out, don't let, don't allow.*

Furthermore, in addition to these *kinds* of appeals, any of them can be intensified by **degree:** get MORE, keep LONGER, change FASTER, avoid MORE, get BETTER, FASTER relief, FEWER problems... and, of course, the hallmark of advertising, the superlatives: BIGGEST, FASTEST, GREATEST, MOST, BEST... Improvement (getting *better*) and growth (getting *bigger*) are related to degree: the fusion of these two concepts (that "bigger *is* better") is quite commonly seen in our culture, although recently it has come under attack from the Schumaker ("Small is beautiful") crowd.

To re-cap this section: one useful way to analyze ads is to focus on our own behaviors as benefit-seekers. For survival and growth, we seek to GET the "good" or KEEP the "good" or CHANGE the "bad" or AVOID the "bad." We should be aware of our own involvement, our own behaviors and desires. We should expect to see all persuasion related to these four basic categories of our needs of *protection* and *acquisition* of the "good," and *relief* and *prevention* of the "bad."

Benefit-Promising

Shift the focus now to the *persuaders* as benefit-promisers and response-seekers. Here are three information-rich statements, any or all of which can be used to analyze persuasion:

(#1) In **behavior,** we can expect persuaders to intensify their own "good" and to downplay their own "bad"; and, in some aggressive or competitive situations, to intensify the others' "bad" and downplay the others' "good."

(#2) In **form,** we can expect this intensifying to be done commonly by means of repetition, association, and composition; and this downplaying to be done commonly by means of omission, diversion, and confusion.

(#3) In **content,** we can expect persuaders to make certain claims about themselves and certain promises of benefits to their audience.

Focus first on the *content* because it's less abstract and easier to illustrate: Persuaders will make certain claims and promises. Claims made by persuaders fall into two categories: claims about *themselves,* and claims about the *intrinsic* merits of their products.

Claims about themselves, made directly or indirectly, explicitly or implicitly, emphasize that the persuaders are competent, trustworthy, and benefit-givers, "on our side." In this book, Chapter 2 ("Trust Me") stresses the *ethos,* or this image projected by the persuaders as a way of building our confidence in them. It is sufficient here to repeat the *benefit-promising* aspect of this image. Basically, the persuader claims to be the *cause* of a desired *effect:* "Trust me, I (my product, my service, my plan, my policy, etc.) will be the *means* by which you will get your desired *end;* I'll help you to *get the good* or to *keep the good* or to *avoid the bad* or to *get rid of the "bad."* There are many different ways in which this is said; for example, it's commonly said more forcefully in directives specifying the response sought: *"in order for you* to get these goods, you *should* buy this, do that, support this, vote for that," and so on.

Claims about the intrinsic merits of the product make up the second major kind of claims. In the following pages, twelve categories are listed which cover nearly every possible claim which can be made about the "good" intrinsic to a product or service. You can expect all (99%?) the product claims you see to fall into these 12 categories: *Superiority, Quantity, Beauty, Efficiency, Scarcity, Novelty, Stability, Reliability, Simplicity, Utility, Rapidity,* and *Safety.*

Each category is illustrated here with a list of "key words" commonly used in advertising. Such lists are descriptive, drawn from observation, based on the rather loose way advertisers actually use words. For example, in the *Superiority* category, words such as "fantastic," "super," "wonderful," and "unbelievable" are listed as expressions common in ads today. Some overlaps occur because of such freewheeling usage, and some omissions may be noted; but, in general, these are the words which have made up the bulk of product claims during the past century and will probably continue to do so for the next. **Opposite each word list is a brief commentary** explaining the category, noting the most common "clusters" of categories, and related products and services.

Furthermore, each category also has a brief listing of **"scare-and-sell"** words, that is, "attack words" relating to the *opposite* undesirable qualities. Although most product claims are positive statements, persuaders can use a negative approach in *any* category by emphasizing the "bad," then offering a solution to the problem. Some people call this "anxiety arousal and satisfaction"; here it's called the "scare-and-sell" technique.

Readers can skim through the following pages, glancing at the word lists, noting the pattern of the commentaries on the opposite pages. However, the *best way* for readers to really comprehend these categories is to take the time to read these lists *aloud,* perhaps even with enthusiasm ("fan-tas-tic!") because the *sound* of these words often triggers our memories, and we'll recall how many times we've heard these words before on the radio or on television. More important, the *next time* we hear these words, we'll pay more attention to the patterns of persuasion, recognize the categories being used, and the options possible.

After you read these lists, look at a magazine advertisement or watch a TV commercial. Notice how quickly you'll pick out these **key words** relating to any product claims. Some simple exercises (such as circling all the key words in a magazine ad) will soon make you very sensitive to these key words, their common clusters, and their limited number of categories. Obviously, you've seen or heard all of these words before, but they've been an *unnoticed verbal environment.* After reading these lists, you become more aware of these patterns of word choice. (In the "white space," add your own examples of new jargon, current slang, and variations.) What's the value of such awareness? **Persuaders want response, not analysis.**

SUPERIORITY

"**Superiority**," as used here, refers to those words which intensify the *high quality* or *excellence* of the product or service. Claims of superiority imply some kind of comparison within the same kind of things. Our language has two special forms of adjectives for this: comparatives (better, more, -er) and superlatives (best, most, -est). Superlatives, especially vague, generalized praise and subjective opinions about *superiority* and *beauty,* are often called *"glittering generalities"* or labeled *"puffery."* (Ads with *specific* comparative claims do exist, but many legal problems involved make this a very complex issue.)

"**Superiority**" words and images (including things *suggested indirectly* by backgrounds, context, music, sounds, metaphors, analogies, examples, and dramatized stories), unlike the other categories listed here, are "all-purpose" praise words which generally can be used with, or clustered with, every other kind of claim.

All products and services use such "**superiority**" words. We assume and expect that everyone will intensify their own "good" when advertising or trying to persuade us. There are very few laws or restrictions against such vague self-praise; the law assumes that most people will recognize and discount such claims as the subjective opinion of the seller.

SCARE AND SELL: "attack words" intensify the opposite undesirable qualities: *poor, bad, shoddy, artificial, inferior, flimsy,* etc.

SUPERIORITY — KEY WORDS

A#1
authentic
best
better
champion
choice
deluxe
excellent
exceptional
expert, expertise
exquisite
extraordinary
fantastic
finest
first class, first-rate
flawless
genuine
good
grand
*greatest
ideal
incredible
incomparable
important
impressive
magnificent
majestic
matchless
memorable
noticeable
outstanding
peerless
perfect
preferable
prize-winning
professional
prominent
quality
real
spectacular
splendid
*super
superb
superior
supreme
top-rate, top-quality
tremendous
unbelievable
unsurpassed
ultimate
ultra-
well-built

QUANTITY

"**Quantity**," as used here, refers to those words which intensify a large *amount* or *number:* in size, space, time, variety of styles, number of services, etc. Emphasis is on plenty, abundance ("more for your money") leading to a very commonly-held idea that "bigger is better." Often, when a large variety is offered, the key verbs will be "choose," "pick," "select" — as if the crucial decision to buy had been made already and now the only issue was the right "choice."

"**Quantity**" words and images (including things *suggested indirectly* by backgrounds, context, music, sounds, metaphors, analogies, examples, and dramatized stories) are often clustered with other categories of related **intrinsic** qualities such as *superiority;* and often with the **"added value"** categories of: *food, economy, popularity, normality, nation, neighborhood, family.*

Products and services often using **"quantity"** words: *"Parity products"* and services, which have very little difference *(drinks, food, cleaning aids);* items with a great variety of *styles (cars, clothes, LPs, books, cameras, stereos, furniture) services (airlines, insurance, stores, banks, credit cards, colleges)* or quantity of *space* involved *(cars, homes, land).*

SCARE AND SELL: "attack words" intensify the opposite undesirable qualities: *skimpy, inadequate, scrawny, too few, too little, lacking, limited,* etc.

Desire-Stimulating

QUANTITY

KEY WORDS

abundant
ample
big
bonus
bountiful
colossal
combines
complete
economy-size
enormous
entire stock
*extra
extra features
family-size
feature-packed
generous supply
giant
gigantic
huge
hundreds of bargains...
immense
includes
jumbo
king-size
large
largest selection...
lush
many
more
more for your money
*most
most choices...
numerous
queen-size
roomy
spacious
stupendous
substantial
super
total coverage
vast
wide variety...

BEAUTY

"**Beauty,**" as used here, refers to those words which intensify the *pleasure* or *delight* provided by, or associated with, the product or service: beautiful objects, people, contexts. The definitions and criteria of beauty may be very subjective, may vary widely; but, everyone will have some set of general "praise words" to talk about "that which being seen, pleases." (Check current teenage slang.)

"**Beauty**" words and images (including things *suggested indirectly* by backgrounds, context, music, sounds, metaphors, analogies, examples, and dramatized stories) are often clustered with other categories of related **intrinsic** qualities such as *superiority, scarcity, stability;* and often with the **"added value"** categories of: *health, activity, sex, elite, nature, neighborhood, intimacy, esteem, generosity.*

Products and services often using "**beauty**" words include: *"body work," cosmetics, clothes, cars, LP records (beautiful sounds), entertainment, (esp. spectacles), travel (to beautiful places), colleges (campus), weddings, homes and land, furniture.*

SCARE AND SELL: "attack words" intensify the opposite undesirable qualities: *ugly, unsightly, revolting, disgusting,* etc.

BEAUTY

KEY WORDS

adorable
attractive
*beautiful
breathtaking
charming
comely
cute
dazzling
delightful
divine
dramatic
dreamy
*elegant
fabulous
fair
glamour
glamorous
good-looking
gorgeous
graceful
heavenly
handsome
*lovely
nice
pretty
striking
stunning
sweet
tasteful
wonderful

EFFICIENCY

"**Efficiency**," as used here, refers to those words which intensify *ability* and *effectiveness: can it* do the job? *does it work?* Often, *strength* and *effort* are related to such efficiency. In one sense, *all* persuaders say or suggest "I am the *means* to the end, the *agent* of the effect"; but, some ads especially emphasize the function of the product or service as a *cause* of a desired effect: e.g., medicines, to stop pain or cure ills; cosmetics, to enhance beauty. (FTC rules require some drug ads to use *qualifiers* — "helps... aids... may relieve... some.")

"**Efficiency**" words and images (including things *suggested indirectly* by backgrounds, context, music, sounds, metaphors, analogies, examples, and dramatized stories) are often clustered with other categories of related **intrinsic** qualities such as *superiority, safety, reliability, utility, rapidity, novelty, simplicity;* and often with the **"added value"** categories of: *health, activity, surroundings, security, sex, science, popularity, normality, completion.*

Products and services often using "**efficiency**" words include: *O-T-C drugs, "body work," cosmetics, cars, car care, cycles, cameras, stereos, airlines, military ads, job ads, self-improvement ads, get-rich-quick ads, home repairs, insurance, baby care, cleaning aids, banks, credit cards.*

SCARE AND SELL: "attack words" intensify the opposite undesirable qualities: *incompetent, unskilled, careless, chaotic, disorganized, weak, lazy,* etc.

EFFICIENCY KEY WORDS

ability
able
adept
aids
capable
careful
competent
deft
diligent
does the job...
*effective
efficient
energetic
fast-acting
hard working
heavy-duty
helps
industrious
organized
potent
*powerful
productive
proficient
qualified
really works...
reinforced
results
rugged
skilled
solid
solution
solves
strong
sturdy
substantial
tough
when results count...
*works

SCARCITY

"**Scarcity**," as used here, refers to those words which intensify that which is *rare* or *infrequent* or in *limited* supply. Scarcity is often linked with the *urgency* appeal: "hurry... only a few left." Although genuine scarcity might relate to only a few basic needs (food, air, shelter), many ads in the affluent society appeal to a common human desire to *collect* trinkets and treasures (coins, stamps, rocks, dishes, pictures). Often, millions of mass-produced "collector's items" are thus sold.

"**Scarcity**" words and images (including things *suggested indirectly* by backgrounds, context, music, sounds, metaphors, analogies, examples, and dramatized stories) are often clustered with other categories of related **intrinsic** qualities such as *superiority, beauty;* and often with the **"added value"** categories of: *elite, intimacy, esteem, generosity, creativity.*

Products and services often using **"scarcity"** words include: *liquor, cosmetics,* some *cars, cameras, stereos, entertainments, college ads, job ads, self-improvement, get-rich-quick ads, real estate, furniture.*

SCARE AND SELL: "attack words" intensify the opposite, undesirable qualities: *commonplace, run of the mill, trite, mundane,* etc.

SCARCITY   KEY WORDS

charter member
collector's item
distinctive
exceptional
*exclusive
first edition
first come, first served
for the first ten customers
hard-to-find
limited edition...
limited supply...
little-known
most treasured
most valued
one of a kind...
*only here, only a few
original
personalized
rare
scarce
seldom seen
singular
sold exclusively at
*special
uncommon
unique
unusual
while supply lasts
your very own

NOVELTY

"Novelty," as used here, refers to those words which intensify the *newness* or *originality* of a product or service. Today, new discoveries and products are very common. One of advertising's major benefits is the *information* which ads give about such new items: people need to be told these new things exist, their benefits, and how to use them.

"Novelty" words and images (including things *suggested indirectly* by backgrounds, context, music, sounds, metaphors, analogies, examples, and dramatized stories) are often clustered with other categories of related **intrinsic** qualities such as *superiority, efficiency, utility, rapidity;* and often with the **"added value"** categories of: *activity, science, play, creativity.*

Products and services often using **"novelty"** words include: *snack foods, "body work," cosmetics, clothes, cars, cameras, stereos, LP records, entertainments, airlines, self-improvement ads, get-rich-quick ads, appliances, cleaning aids.*

SCARE AND SELL: "attack words" intensify the opposite undesirable qualities: *outdated, worn out, passe, obsolete,* etc.

NOVELTY   KEY WORDS

advanced
all new
amazing new
announcing
breakthrough
contemporary
discovery
*exciting new
fashion
fashionable
first showing
fresh
future
futuristic
introducing
introductory offer
incredible new
just released
latest
modern
modernistic
*new improved
novel
now
original
premier
progressive
recent
remarkable new
revolutionary new
state-of-the-art
style
stylish
timely
today's
up-to-date

STABILITY

"**Stability**," as used here, refers to those words which intensify a favorable sense of the *old* and the *past*, a "conservative" appeal, especially in contrast to a "progressive" praise of the new and the modern. In our mobile "rootless" society, the "search for roots" has a strong appeal, often reflected in ad campaigns.

"**Stability**" words and images (including things *suggested indirectly* by backgrounds, context, music, sounds, metaphors, analogies, examples, and dramatized stories) are often clustered with other categories of related **intrinsic** qualities such as: *superiority, beauty, reliability;* and often with the **"added value"** *categories of: religion, nature, nation, neighborhood, intimacy, family, belonging, esteem.*

Products and services often using "**stability**" words include: some *foods, beer, liquor, cars, cameras, furniture (esp. antiques), old hotels, traditional colleges, some older homes, established repair services, established insurance agents, older retail stores,* and *mail order firms, banks, corporations,* and *services associated with traditional family ceremonies and rituals* (weddings, funerals, confirmations, bar mitzvahs).

SCARE AND SELL: "attack words" intensify the opposite undesirable qualities: *untested, untried, inexperienced, new-fangled,* etc.

STABILITY　　　　　　　　　　　　　KEY WORDS

    aged
    ancient
    antique
   *classic
    classic styling
    conservation
    conserve
    continuous
    established
    ever since (date)
    experienced
    for over _____ years
    fully developed
    heritage
    historic
    historical
    history
    mature
    nostalgia
    nostalgic
    old family recipe
    old-fashioned
    old style
    old world
    past
    permanent
    preserve
    proven
    ripe
    ripened
    seasoned
    stabile
    time-tested
    tradition
    traditional
    tried and true
    unchanging
    yesteryear

RELIABILITY

"**Reliability**," as used here, refers to those words which intensify the *predictability* and *sameness* of a product or service. Such reliability can relate either to *time (same* results from *repeated* use) or to *space (same* qualities in all of the *parts):* any emphasis on *brand names* or *franchise names:* e.g., "The best surprise is no surprise at all "(Holiday Inn);" "You expect more from Standard, and you get it"; "You can be sure if it's Westinghouse."

"**Reliability**" words and images (including things *suggested indirectly* by backgrounds, context, music, sounds, metaphors, analogies, examples, and dramatized stories) are closely related to the basic "confidence" appeal (in which the speaker/seller asks the buyer to "trust me"), and often clustered with other categories of related **intrinsic** qualities such as *superiority, efficiency, stability, safety, utility, simplicity;* often with the **"added value"** categories of: *health, surroundings, security, science, popularity, normality, family, esteem.*

Products and services often using **"reliability"** words include: *"body work,"* clothes, cars, cameras, hotels, airlines, home repairs, utilities, insurance, baby care, cleaning aids, banks.

SCARE AND SELL: "attack words" intensify the opposite undesirable qualities: *untrustworthy, unreliable, unpredictable, erratic, etc.*

RELIABILITY   KEY WORDS

always ready
authorized dealer
bonded
*dependable
durable
endurance
enduring
equal
equivalent
expected
*experienced
faithful
firm
fixed
identical
lasting
licensed
long-lasting
permanent
predictable
*reliable
repeated
same
secure
solid
stable
standard
steadfast
steady
trustworthy
unchanging
uniform

SIMPLICITY

"**Simplicity**," as used here, refers to those words which intensify the *easy* and *uncomplicated* aspects of a product or service. The stress here is on being *without* effort, hardness, difficulty, or problems; not only in using it, but also in buying, maintaining, etc. In our society (which has myths about the virtues of doing hard work, overcoming difficulties) some ads "give permissions" for such ease and convenience by stressing it as a reward for past goodness ("You deserve a break today") or stressing the positive aspects of time-saving, labor-saving.

"**Simplicity**" words and images (including things *suggested indirectly* by backgrounds, context, music, sounds, metaphors, analogies, examples, and dramatized stories) are often clustered with other categories of related **intrinsic** qualities such as *superiority, efficiency, rapidity, utility, reliability;* and often with the "**added value**" categories of: *health, food, activity, surroundings, sex, economy, popularity, normality, family, completion.*

Products and services often using "**simplicity**" words include: *cereals, snack foods, easy-foods, fast-foods, O-T-C drugs, "body work," clothes, car care, cameras, hotels, airlines, job ads, self-improvement ads, get-rich-quick ads, home repairs, baby care, toys, cleaning aids, banks, credit cards.*

SCARE AND SELL: "attack words" intensify the opposite undesirable qualities: *difficult, hard, complex, complicated, problems, worry,* etc.

SIMPLICITY   KEY WORDS

added convenience
all-expenses-paid
all-included
anyone can learn
automatic
beginner's
billed later
built-in
carefree
child's play
complete with
*convenient
convenient monthly payments
comprehensive
delivered direct
*easy
easy-care
easy-handling
easy-to-follow instructions
effortless
energy-saving
ez
fingertip control
foolproof
hassle-free
instant
just charge it...
labor-saving
learn at home
maintenance-free
no moving parts
one step
only minutes a day
problem-free
pushbutton ease
ready to wear
*simple
self-contained
self-storing
shipped automatically
smooth
step-by-step instructions
time-saving
trouble-free
virtually no effort

UTILITY

"Utility," as used here, refers to those words which intensify the *usefulness* and *versitility* of the product or service, usually as a *means* to do something else.

"**Utility**" words and images (including things *suggested indirectly* by backgrounds, context, music, sounds, metaphors, analogies, examples, and dramatized stories) are often clustered with other categories of related **intrinsic** qualities such as *superiority, reliability, simplicity, efficiency, quantity, novelty;* and often with the "**added value**" of: *food, activity, surroundings, economy, popularity, normality, family, generosity.*

Products and services often using "**utility**" words include: *easy-foods, fast-foods, "body work," clothes, cars, car care, cameras, home repairs, appliances, baby care, toys, cleaning aids, credit cards.*

SCARE AND SELL: "attack words" intensify the opposite undesirable qualities: *useless, limited, worthless, impractical,* etc.

UTILITY

KEY WORDS

adjustable
all-around
all-in-one
all purpose
basic outfit
combination
compatible
convertible
detachable
double-duty
down-to-earth
dozens of uses
essential
fully-equipped
functional
go-anywhere
goes with anything
interchangeable
many-sided
mix and match
multi-purpose
portable
*practical
precise
re-cycle
resourceful
re-usable
reversable
sensible
suitable
three-in-one
useful
universal
variable
versitile
washable

RAPIDITY

"**Rapidity**," as used here, refers to those words which intensify the *speed* of a product or service. In most cases, a fast rate of speed is desirable, especially when the product or service is a *means to an end:* For example, quick-acting medicine, fast jet travel, fast-food service. In some cases, a deliberate slowness is desirable, especially when the product or service is *an end in itself:* for example, a leisurely ocean voyage, or an elaborate restaurant dinner.

"**Rapidity**" words and images (including things *suggested directly* by backgrounds, context, music, sounds, metaphors, analogies, examples, and dramatized stories) are often clustered with other categories of related **intrinsic** qualities such as *superiority, efficiency, novelty, simplicity;* and often with the **"added value"** categories of: *health, food, activity, economy, completion.*

Products and services often using "**rapidity**" words include: *cereals, easy-foods, fast-foods, O-T-C drugs, "body work," cars, car care, cycles, cameras, airlines, job ads, home repairs, baby care, cleaning aids.*

SCARE AND SELL: "attack words" intensify the opposite undesirable qualities: if desired pace is fast, then *"slow,"* and *"sluggish,"* would be attack words; if desired pace is calm, leisurely, then *"rushed"* and *"hurried"* would be attack words.

RAPIDITY　　　　　　　　　　　　　　KEY WORDS

If a fast speed is desirable:
brisk
fast
*instant
jiffy
prompt
quick
*rapid
ready
speedy
sudden
swift

If a slow speed is desirable:
calm
deliberate
leisurely
long lasting
relaxed
restful
slow
slow burning
time-released

SAFETY

"**Safety,**" as used here, refers to those words which intensify the *safe* and *harmless* qualities of the product or service itself. Such safety words are commonly backed up today by testimonials by various certifying authorities: Good Housekeeping "Seal of Approval"; Underwriter's Laboratory (UL); FDIC insured; FDA's "Generally Regarded As Safe" (GRAS) list.

"**Safety**" words and images (including things *suggested indirectly* by backgrounds, context, music, sounds, metaphors, analogies, examples, and dramatized stories) are often clustered with other categories of related **intrinsic** qualities such as *superiority, reliability, efficiency;* and often with the "**added value**" categories of: *health, surroundings, security, family.*

Products and services often using "**safety**" words include: *food, medicines, "body work," cleaning aids, baby care, toys, insurance, banks, nursing homes,* etc.

SCARE AND SELL: "attack words" intensify the opposite, undesirable qualities: *unsafe, dangerous, harmful, poisonous, breakable,* etc.

SAFETY KEY WORDS

additive-free
burglarproof
care
careful
certain
childproof
fail-safe
fireproof
fire-resistant
fire-retardant
guard
guaranteed
harmless
immune
nonflammable
protected
pure
resists
rest assured
risk-free
*safe
safeguarded
shatter proof
shielded
sure
tested
unadulterated
uncontaminated
unpolluted
withstands
worry-free

OTHER WAYS

There are other ways of looking at claims in advertising. For example, if the message focuses on the **maker** (the source, the company, the manufacturer), it's predictable that the commonly repeated words will relate to the cluster of *Superiority* ("the best"), *Quantity* ("the largest"), *Stability* ("the oldest"), and *Reliability* ("trusted"). The usual message about the **material** or the **design** will focus on *Superiority* ("best"), *Quantity* ("most"), *Beauty* ("beautiful"), *Scarcity* ("rare"), *Novelty* ("new"), *Stability* ("classic"), *Reliability* ("dependable"), and Safety ("safe"). The usual message about the **use** focuses on *Efficiency* ("really works"), *Utility* ("useful"), *Rapidity* ("fast-acting"), *Simplicity* ("easy"), and Safety ("safe").

Perhaps the *simplest* way of talking about advertising claims is merely to list the most commonly repeated words. Many books have offered such lists, usually based on some informed estimates. Some will claim that *"free"* is the magic word; others will swear that it's the combination *"exciting new."* For what it's worth, here's a list:

15 MOST-REPEATED ADVERTISING CLAIMS

"exciting new"	(activity/novelty)
"fast acting"	(rapidity/efficiency)
"greatest"	(superiority)
"most"	(quantity)
"best"	(superiority)
"classic"	(stability)
"beautiful"	(beauty)
"only"	(scarcity)
"easy"	(simplicity)
"practical"	(utility)
"free"	(economy)
"less than"	(economy)
"earn"	(economy)
"save"	(economy)
"take advantage of"	(economy)

To re-cap: people are benefit-seekers; they seek to *keep* or *get* the "good" and *get rid of* or *avoid* the "bad." These relationships can be applied to *any* kind of "good" or "bad," whether we're talking about an intrinsic "good" inherent in the product, (such as superiority, quantity, beauty, efficiency, scarcity, novelty, stability, reliability, simplicity, utility, rapidity, safety) or an "added value" associated with the product.

Associations: "Added Values"

In most cases, the promised benefits are *never explicitly promised,* yet they are strongly implied. Sometimes these associations are neither true nor logical, yet the technique is effective.

The association technique basically links three elements together: (1) the product or idea, with (2) something *already held favorably by or desired by* (3) the intended audience.

The pattern is the same, but the middle element is reversed in the "scare-and-sell" version of this technique (and in "attack" propaganda): the persuader associates (1) the product or idea, with (2) something *already disliked or feared by* (3) the intended audience.

Thus, persuaders must first know what the intended audience likes and dislikes. What *do* people need? Want or desire? No one knows for certain. There's no absolute, fixed list of human needs. Philosophers and psychologists have long tried to analyze such human motivation and behavior. More recently, advertisers and market researchers have spent billions in a search to find out what people like and dislike, why people act.

Such **"market research"** (also called "consumer behavior research," motivational research," "audience analysis," etc.) is a very important part of the persuasion process. Not all individuals or groups will respond the same way, but researchers seek predictable patterns of behavior by studying specific audiences. What's a "good thing" for one audience may be a "bad thing" for another: ads in *Playboy* are geared differently than those in *Good Housekeeping.* Advertisers try to target a specific audience — by age, sex, race, occupation, income, area, etc., which can be easily measured.

Advertisers thus spend millions each year in opinion polls, surveys, questionnaires, sociological and psychological studies to find out what motivates human behavior, what people like and dislike. Although this extensive research has not produced *exact* answers, we do know enough to predict *probably* patterns and *common* reasons for human behavior.

Here's a very useful "common sense" list of human needs, illustrated with examples from contemporary advertising. These categories are *general and abstract;* the actual stimulus will be *specific and concrete.* *"Sex,"* for example, is a general category here, but an ad may show the *smile* of a *beautiful woman.* Such a listing doesn't attempt to create a rigidly fixed classification system: certainly some categories and examples can be questioned. But, the basic principle remains that some human hopes and fears are known and predictable. Advertisers, in their very practical way, are not too interested whether these are *universal* needs or "merely" *very common* ones.

NEEDS, WANTS, & DESIRES
— *A Useful List:*

Basic Needs
Food
Activity
Surroundings
Sex
Health
Security
Economy

A Sense of Certitude & Approval
Religion
Science
Best People
Most People
Average People

A Sense of Space & Territory
Neighborhood
Nation
Nature

A Sense of Love & Belonging
Intimacy
Family
Groups

Other Growth Needs
Esteem
Play
Generosity
Curiosity
Creativity
Completion

— A Brief Comment:

Basic Needs
People have basic needs, essential for survival. Food and water are obviously essential to individual survival, as sex is essential to the continuation of the species. But a livable "air bubble," physical activity, a healthy body, a safe environment, are also vital for human life. In a civilized society, money ("Economy") is so closely related, as a *means,* to basic survival goals, that it is included here.

A Sense of Certitude & Approval
People seek *emotional security,* support and reassurance from outside sources that we are doing right, that the world makes sense. Such a stabile worldview was once provided by a church, state, or a social order, but today there is a lack of commonly-shared faith. To judge by the number of *testimonials, endorsements,* and *authority figures* used in ads, today there seems to be a strong desire for outside re-assurance.

A Sense of Space & Territory
People have a sense of space or territoriality, a possessive relationship of the space about them. This can be imagined in terms of layers, or ripples, extending outward from the self: starting with close *"personal space"* ("my seat... my room... my house"), extending to the *neighborhood* (region, hometown, etc.) one knows firsthand and to the artificial political boundaries of a *nation,* and finally to our relationship with the whole world of *nature.*

A Sense of Love & Belonging
People have a need to belong, to love and to be loved, to be related to others in bonds of mutual care, and to have a sense of "relatedness" to others, and "rootedness" in a family or a group. Such social bonding involves human relationships with relatives, friends, and in groups.

Other Growth Needs
Human behavior cannot be explained simply in terms of basic survival needs. Once people have satisfied certain basic needs, there are other human desires. Even though such "higher" needs or "growth" needs are hard to define or classify, there's common agreement that people are motivated by such higher aspirations.

Manipulating Human Hopes and Fears, Dreams and Nightmares

Before looking at the specific categories, some general commentary may be useful to point up some qualifications (concerning mix, degree, options) and some practical problems (concerning inequality, conflict, frustration, dissatisfaction, and fear) which are related to this whole business of manipulating human hopes and fears. Today, in a society in which thousands of professional persuaders intensify some specific human needs, *for their own benefit,* our sanity and mental health depends upon our awareness of this situation. As we look at some of the techniques of the benefit-promisers, we should also be aware of our roles as the benefit-seekers.

Mix. *"Different Strokes for Different Folks."* People have many needs, wants, desires, dreams, and hopes. But, although we share much in common, everyone has a different mix. Even though we can talk about certain common clusters of things which tend to go together, everyone has a unique "package."

Degree. Not every "need" on this list will be desired by everyone in the same *degree*. Sometimes we focus on *one* (or a few) of our possible needs and desires. Any need can be very intense, especially in a crisis. We are seldom aware of breathing, for example, unless we are suffocating. "To a starving man," the old adage goes, "food is God." Any unfulfilled desire can be *obsessive* if we devote a great degree of attention and a great amount of time and emotional energy to it. We speak of people being obsessed with *sexual desire* (or *money* or *power)* or of being overwhelmed with *grief* (or *fear* or *loneliness),* or of being *too dependent* upon the approval of others. Such intensity of emotion fixed on *one* aspect of human needs can be seen in the patriot who dies for a country, the martyr who dies for a cause or a religious faith, the lover who is in despair because of being rejected by the beloved, the homesick person far away from familiar places, and so on.

Options. Not every single desire must be satisfied. We are flexible, adaptable. We can compromise, make adjustments, trade-offs. When some things are denied to us, out of our reach, beyond our potential, we can direct our energy elsewhere. We can compensate, we can sublimate, we can re-direct. If one desire can't be fulfilled, we don't have to be stalled, hung up, immobilized.

Inequality. There's nothing wrong *per se,* nothing intrinsically bad, with persuaders defining and analyzing their audience's needs and wants. It's reasonable for example, if advertisers are going to spend money to persuade others, the most economical and effective ways will be used. Part of a persuader's overall strategy includes an analysis of the attitudes of the intended audience, of those things *already* held by the audience. In our own person-to-person communication, we all do the same thing — but in a rather amateurish, inefficient way — as we try to "size up" or "psych out" or understand the wants and needs of the other person. The critical difference is the state of *inequality* today between the professional persuaders and the average person. Not only do the persuaders have the money, machines, and the media access, but also they've rented many of the best psychiatrists and professors of psychology and sociology as consultants.

Children and teen-agers, for example, do not recognize that many of their emotional crises, their hopes and fears, are quite predictable. Just as a baby book can predict the physical development of the child with great accuracy, so also a great deal is predictable about emotional development. Children are inexperienced and usually unable to view themselves in a detached fashion as an adult would. But even with advertising directed at adults, inequality also exists because most adults are not *as skilled* or *as trained* in persuasion techniques, or in the psychology of human behavior, as those professional persuaders in our society. Very few adults will admit to this. Most people are vain. The most common adult reaction is a grand assertion: "advertising doesn't affect *me*... I *never* buy anything just because I saw it on TV." But, effective persuasion does have an impact on us. And the more we recognize the patterns and techniques of persuasion, the less inequality there will be between the persuaders and the persuadees.

We need to recognize our own dreams, our hopes, our fantasies and desires: we want to belong, to be loved, to be happy, to be rich, to lead the good life, to do something, to be famous. We also need to recognize our own fears and nightmares: we don't want to be lonely, to be rejected, to be poor, to be confused, to have pain. But, we seldom think about these things *systematically* or precisely. We often get involved in the process or details of one specific dream or nightmare, or we often shift back and forth in the cross-currents of daily living.

Yet the professional persuaders know that these hopes and fears exist in us and are rather systematic in their manipulation of them. If advertisers are often accused of peddling dreams, we must recognize first that they are *our* dreams: they are all genuine human desires; they are the benefits we seek.

Few people seldom encourage us to recognize *all* of our needs and wants: advertisers usually focus in on *one* relating to their specific transaction, and other persuaders (including religious, political, and social persuaders) often criticize our needs which *compete* with *their* transactions: "you *shouldn't* be materialistic... you *shouldn't* want that... you *should* spend your money and time doing *this* instead..." Certainly, persuaders do have the right to criticize competing value systems, yet we can be aware that most of our lives we've been subject to persuasion attempts emphasizing some specific categories and criticising others. Every "cause" (like every product) is likely to seek priority for itself.

Persuaders *don't create* human needs. Without a single ad, people would still eat, drink, breathe, move, make love, seek friends and esteem. But, persuaders can intensify the focus, can try to channel our desires toward some specific ends. This multiplicity and complexity of human desires can cause many psychological problems for us.

Conflicts. Sometimes we can't decide what's more important. Seldom we have an easy decision between the obvious good and the obvious bad; usually we have to choose between *the greater of two goods,* or *the lesser of two evils.* In the past, church and state often assigned some clear goals and guidelines for behavior: *religious* duty, the goal was Heaven, attained by leading the "good life"; *secular duty,* the goal was service to the country or the system, attained by "doing one's job well," following orders, or "meeting one's quota." Such obligations and duties imposed by others created a clear sense of goals and things we *"should"* seek. Today, some of these guidelines have broken down, and advertising acts as a new outside force suggesting others *goals* ("You'll be *happy...* ") and the *ways* to achieve them ("...if you *buy* our product."). We cannot get everything we want, nor in the degree we want. We have to choose what, and in what order. We need to select, to be aware of our options and the pressures around us.

Frustrations. There are many things we simply can't have, or can't do. We don't have enough money or time or talent. We are limited, unable, incapable. We have to make judgments about those things which are within our personal, individual potency. Ads directed at a large audience often are received by many people who are *not* the advertiser's target audience. While advertisers might regard such overlap as minor waste, or unavoidable "spillage" useless to them, the cumulative effect of people being stimulated by many things outside their potential can lead to personal frustrations. Borderline cases often appear in a credit-card economy. With easy credit and loans available, the borderline between the possible and the impossible is blurred. Millions of people are deep in debt-cycles because there has been a blurring of what they really can afford and what they can't.

Dissatisfactions. People can *desire* only that which they do *not* have; once they get it, they can be either *satisfied* or *not satisfied.* If things do not live up to expectations, anticipations, or idealized fantasies, then people can be dissatisfied, disappointed, disillusioned. Dissatisfaction is expecially common when desires are *intensely* stimulated, with great promises and puffery. Although most advertising seeks to stimulate *desire,* some ads encourage *satisfaction* with the product already purchased, either to retain *"brand loyalty"* for repeat purchases (cars, cigarettes, foods, etc.) or to get customers to stimulate *others'* desire by word-of-mouth referrals.

Fears. For every human need, desire, hope or dream, there's a corresponding fear or nightmare. While it is normal to have such fears, they can be intensified deliberately by others. Sometimes persuaders manipulate such fears to sell a product: "anxiety arousal and satisfaction"; that is, the persuader seeks to arouse a fear, then promise a relief to the threat; a problem is emphasized, then a solution offered. In this book, the term *"scare-and-sell"* is used to describe this technique, and some examples of it are given in every category discussing human needs. Although *fear* is frequently common in political and religious propaganda, it is used *relatively less* in commercial advertising (where sunshine and smiles predominate), thus it receives less attention here.

Too Much of a Good Thing. Generally speaking, "scare-and-sell' words are directly contradictory to the "good" things: if something is "good," then "too little" (the *lack,* the *omission,* the *absence)* of it is "bad." However, we also have some attack words concerning *excessive degree: "too much"* of a good thing.

Perhaps these words refer more precisely to *an abuse, a misuse* of a good thing, or to a *false appearance* (pretense, facade, illusion) of a "good." For example, people have certain needs and desires for food, for belonging, for esteem; however, we also recognize that these desires, carried to an *excessive* degree, lead to gluttony, dependency, and vanity.

Relatively speaking, there are fewer words to attack an excess of a good thing, and they tend to be less common, more atypical. We *borrow* words from other languages ("chauvinist," "provincial"); we use *metaphors* ("clinging vine," "apron strings," "umbilical cord" — for excessive need to belong) and *allusions* ("Frankenstein's monster" — for an abuse of scientific knowledge, "Machiavellian" — for an abuse of political power; "pharisees" and "zealots" — for excesses or abuses of religious attitudes), and *made-up- words* ("goof-off," "artsy," "palsy-walsy" — for abuses concerning play, creativity, friendship).

Even in such qualities as "health" and "beauty" which seem so *absolute,* so *universally desired,* we can make up "attack words" (such as "health-nut") or use quotation marks in writing ("beauty") or the tone of our voice to indicate our attack. We do hear people saying things such as "she was too beautiful for her own good," implying that "excessive" beauty may have a cluster of related problems, unpleasant side-effects. The woman who is "too beautiful" may be vain, egocentric, inconsiderate of others; or she may receive the unwanted, uninvited attentions of those attracted by her beauty.

Attack words concerning *excessive* degree will *not* be listed in the "scare-and-sell" boxes which focus on the most common situations, but this is a reminder here that *any* quality can be praised or criticized.

▶ Add your own examples in the "white space" of new jargon, current slang, and variations.

FOOD

"**Food**" is used here as a category of some human need or desire, a "good thing" *already* wanted or desired by people; ads often *simply associate* their product or service with "**food**" words and images, thus *suggesting* or *implying* "added value" to the buyer.

Food is basic. Even without advertising, people still eat. But the function of an ad is to direct our appetite toward a *particular* product, a *specific kind* of food or a *certain* brand. Taste is subjective, learned or acquired from many sources. Ads try to persuade us that their product has the taste (texture, smell) we like. Target audience for food ads used to be limited to the "homemaker" (often, the mother); but now, more snack-foods and fast-food ads are directed at children.

"**Food**" words and images (including things *suggested indirectly* by backgrounds, context, music, sounds, metaphors, analogies, examples, and dramatized stories) are often clustered with other categories of human **needs and desires,** such as *activity, health, economy, nature, family;* and often with words stressing **intrinsic** qualities such as *superiority, quantity, utility, rapidity, simplicity* of such **products and services** as: *soft drinks, candy, cereals, snack foods, baby foods, easy-foods, fast-food restuarants,* etc.

SCARE AND SELL: "attack words" intensify the opposite, undesirable aspects: the lack of good tasting food; *bland, dull, tasteless, unappetizing, harsh, bitter, etc.*

FOOD KEY WORDS

appealing
appetizing
banquet
chewy
creamy
crispy
crunchy
cuisine
delectable
delicate
delicious
feast
flavorful
full-bodied
gourmet
homecooking
juicy
lucious
mouth-watering
rich
robust
savory
scrumptuous
smooth
spicy
sweet
tangy
tempting
tasty
tender
well-seasoned
zesty

ACTIVITY

"Activity" is used here as a category of some human need or desire, a "good thing" *already* wanted or desired by people; ads often *simply associate* their product or service with **"activity"** words and images, thus *suggesting* or *implying* an "added value" to the buyer.

People need to be active. Our *senses,* our *muscles* need to be stimulated, to be used. Such activity, motion, and response is basic to life. Experiments in "sensory deprivation," in which people are cut off from all sense-input, demonstrate the importance of such vital activities. (Sleep and rest, in alternate periods, are also essential to the rhythm of life.) *Nonverbal* associations commonly used stress movement, motion, repetition, intensity, variety in music and visual images (e.g., hard-driving rock music, stirring march music, powerful symphonic music; flashing lights, bright colors; moving in patterns-bands, parades, dancers, etc.).

"Activity" words and images (including things *suggested indirectly* by backgrounds, context, music, sounds, metaphors, analogies, examples, and dramatized stories) are often clustered with other categories of human **needs and desires,** such as *sex, food, health, esteem, play;* and often with words stressing **intrinsic** qualities such as *superiority, beauty, efficiency, rapidity,* and *reliability* of such **products and services** as: *foods, drinks, cosmetics, clothes, "body work," entertainments, vacations, travel,* etc.

SCARE AND SELL: "attack words" intensify the opposite, undesirable aspects: the lack of activity; *inert, passive, dull, lazy, lethargic, inactive, feeble, senile,* etc.

Desire-Stimulating

ACTIVITY

action
action-packed
active
activity
adventure
adventurous
agile
agility
alert
alertness
alive
animated
bouyant
brisk
bubbling
busy
dynamic
energetic
energy
enthusiastic
*exciting
lively
nimble
perky
quick
radiant
robust
sparkling
sprightly
spry
thrilling
vibrant
vigor
vigorous
vital
vitality
vivacious
young
youth
youthful
wide-awake

KEY WORDS

REST, RELAXATION words:
calm
calming
gentle
mild
peace
peaceful
quiet
refresh
refreshing
relax
relaxing
serene
serenity
soothe
soothing
tranquil
tranquility

SURROUNDINGS

"**Surroundings**" is used here as a category of some human need or desire, a "good thing" *already* wanted or desired by people; ads often *simply associate* their product or service with "**surroundings**" words and images, thus *suggesting* or *implying* an "added value" to the buyer.

People have an absolute need for an "air bubble" with *adequate oxygen, within certain temperature* ranges. We seldom notice our surroundings or environment until threat appears, usually in terms of *extremely hot* or *cold* weather. More recently, we have been threatened with air pollution (smog, ozone alerts, etc.) and radiation. Even when the extremes are avoided, there are *degrees* of comfort and pleasantness in our surroundings. *Smells* can penetrate our "air bubble" in a way that sights and sounds cannot: at times, pleasant (some perfume scents, some cooking aromas); at times, unpleasant ("Smoking stinks!").

"**Surroundings**" words and images (including things *suggested indirectly* by backgrounds, context, music, sounds, metaphors, analogies, examples, and dramatized stories) are often clustered with other categories of human **needs and desires,** such as *nature* and *neighborhood;* and often with words stressing **intrinsic** qualities such as *superiority, safety* and *efficiency* of such **products and services** as: *clothes, homes, travel (winter vacations), heating and cooling, appliances,* etc.

SCARE AND SELL: "attack words" intensify the opposite, undesirable aspects: the lack of moderate surroundings; *searing sun, scorching, sweltering heat; icy blasts, bone chilling cold, biting cold, foul weather, subzero, freezing, foul air, smog,* etc.

SURROUNDINGS   **KEY WORDS**

aroma
bundle up
cool
cooling
comfort
comfortable
cozy
fragrant
*fresh
livable
mellow
mild
pure
scent
smooth
soft
warm
warmth
windbreaker

SEX

"**Sex**" is used here as a category of some human need or desire, a "good thing" *already* wanted or desired by people; ads often *simply associate* their product or service with "**sex**" words and images, thus *suggesting* or *implying* an "added value" to the buyer.

Sex is an intensely popular, pleasurable, pre-occupation with most people; thus, ads are quite likely to use as many sexual associations as the norms of a society tolerate (Ads in some European countries are *more* overtly sexual, in Arab countries much *less* so, than in the USA.) Sexual associations tend to be vague, indirect, suggestive, pleasantly romanticized (young beauties) often appealing to our own desire to be more attractive, desirable to others (by purchasing the product!) *Words* are "soft" (*vulgar* words are rarely used), but *nonverbals* (esp. pictures) are the most commonly-used ways of association. Some critics claim that a "subliminal seduction" can occur with ads using "secret" sexual messages implanted; however, such a "conspiracy theory" diverts attention from our own genuine interest in sex, our own responsible choice, and the very obvious fact that ads try to associate their product with many other human needs and desires.

"**Sex**" words and images (including things *suggested indirectly* by backgrounds, context, music, sounds, metaphors, analogies, examples, and dramatized stories) are often clustered with other categories of human **needs and desires,** such as *activity, intimacy, esteem, play, curiosity;* and often with words stressing **intrinsic** qualities such as *superiority, beauty, simplicity,* of such **products and services** as *"body work," cosmetics, clothes, cars, wedding* (honeymoon), etc.

SCARE AND SELL: "attack words" intensify the opposite, undesirable aspects: the lack of sexual fullfillment; *frigid, impotent, undesirable, unattractive,* etc.

SEX

KEY WORDS

affectionate
allure
alluring
amorous
attractive
beauty
beautiful
beloved
carnal
desirable
desire
earthly
enticing
erotic
feminine
love
lover
lusty
manly
masculine
passion
passionate
provacative
romance
romantic
seductive
sensual
sexy
stimulating
virile

HEALTH

"**Health**" is used here as a category of some human need or desire, a "good thing" *already* wanted or desired by people; ads often *simply associate* their product or service with "**health**" words and images, thus *suggesting* or *implying* an "added value" to the buyer.

Good health is desired by all. When Aristotle wrote about "appearance" and "reality," he commented that most people would be content with the *appearance* of virtue, but wanted the *reality* of health. People seek to sustain life and to avoid pain. Although we know that pain is a protective warning signal to the body, most people would prefer an easier way of getting such information. When we're healthy, we're seldom aware of the *absence* of pain and often indifferent to protecting our health; but when we're sick or in pain, we place a very high priority on stopping pain, on getting better. Relief from pain is one of the most powerful human desires; ads related to this must be very carefully considered.

"**Health**" words and images (including things *suggested indirectly* by backgrounds, context, music, sounds, metaphors, analogies, examples, and dramatized stores) are often clustered with other categories of human **needs and desires,** such as *food, activity, security, family,* and *science;* and often with words stressing **intrinsic** qualities such as *superiority, efficiency, rapidity, safety, beauty,* and *reliability* of such **products and services** as some *foods, drugs* and *medicines,* some *clothes,* some *travel, "body work," baby care items,* some *cleaning aids, insurance,* etc.

SCARE AND SELL: "attack words" intensify the opposite, undesirable aspects: the lack of good health; *pain, suffering, unclean, dirty, unhealthy, sick, ill,* etc.

HEALTH
KEY WORDS

aids
alleviate the pain
assists
beneficial
benefits
clean
cures
growth
heals
health
healthful
healthy
hygenic
hygiene
relief
relieves discomfort
remedy
restores
sanitary
well being

SECURITY

"**Security**" is used here as a category of some human need or desire, a "good thing" *already* wanted or desired by people; ads often *simply associate* their product or service with "**security**" words and images, thus *suggesting* or *implying* an "added value" to the buyer.

People seek security, protection from danger and threats ("to avoid the 'bad' "), as part of our basic need for self-preservation. As social animals, humans have organized societies for their mutual self-protection; often such function of their police and military is reflected in the language (National *Guard,* Department of *Defense,* "national *security"*) and "security" language is likely to be common in social and political persuasion. But, commercial advertising also uses this language because there are many threats and dangers possible, and governmental protection is often limited or ineffective.

"**Security**" words and images (including things *suggested indirectly* by backgrounds, context, music, sounds, metaphors, analogies, examples, and dramatized stories) are often clustered with other categories of human **needs and desires,** such as *health, science, family, generosity;* and often with words stressing **intrinsic** qualities such as *efficiency, superiority, reliability, economy,* and *safety* of such **products and services** as *medicine, "body work,"* some *cosmetics, cars, homes, home repairs, insurance, baby care,* some *cleaning aids, banks, credit cards,* and some specific devices, such as *guns, locks, fences, alarms, CB radios,* etc.

SCARE AND SELL: "attack words" intensify the opposite, undesirable aspects: the lack of security; *accident, tragedy, disaster, calamity, loss, death,* etc.

SECURITY   KEY WORDS

cover
defend
foresight
freedom from worry
guard
peace of mind
prevent
prevention
protect
protection
resist
safe
safeguard
safety
secure
security
shield
take care of
withstand

ECONOMY

"**Economy**" is used here as a category of some human need or desire, a "good thing" *already* wanted or desired by people; ads often *simply associate* their product or service with "**economy**" words and images, thus *suggesting* or *implying* an "added value" to the buyer.

Although money "can't buy happiness," it can buy some of the basic human needs (food, shelter, etc.) and perhaps some pleasures in life. Money is a *means* to material goods; material goods are often presented as a *means* to non-material goods (esteem, belonging, etc.) Thus, most folks seek to get more money and try to keep or protect what they have. Even when we are asked to *spend,* ads emphasize that we are *saving,* a paradox explained by other *implied* factors such as "value," "investment," or comparative relationship ("all things considered"). Most ads downplay any hidden costs (upkeep, repairs, extras) and assure us of the wisdom of our purchase. *Get-rich-quick* schemes and *con games* exploit the human desire to get more money; gambling (lotteries, sweepstakes, contests, prizes) also appeals to a passive dream of easy money. *Any* "give away," "discount," "rebate" relates to this category.

"**Economy**" words and images (including things *suggested indirectly* by backgrounds, context, music, sounds, metaphors, analogies, examples, and dramatized stories) are often clustered with other categories of human **needs and desires,** such as *safety;* and often with words stressing **intrinsic** qualities such as *superiority, quantity, utility, rapidity,* and *simplicity* of such **products and services** as *soft drinks,* some *foods,* some *clothes,* some *cars,* book clubs, some *travel* (packaged tours), *job ads,* some *homes and land, home repairs,* some *furniture,* some *insurance plans,* some *retail stores* (discount houses), *cleaning aids,* etc.

SCARE AND SELL: "attack words" intensify the opposite, undesirable aspects: the lack of money; *loss, being cheated, overcharged, taken advantage of* by others, etc.

ECONOMY　　　　　　　　　　　　　　　　KEY WORDS

   afford, affordable
*bargain
*budget, budget-priced
   cheap
   discount
   down-to-earth prices
   earn, earnings
   economy, economical
   for as little as...
*free, free offer, free sample
   frugal
   gain
   gift
   giveaway
   half-price
   included free
   inexpensive
   invest, investment
   jackpot
*just
*less than...
   low cost
   lowest possible...
   modestly priced
   money-saving
   more for your money
   no extra cost
*only...
   penny-pinchers
   prices cut
   prize
   profit, profitable
   reasonably priced
   rebate
   refund
   reduced
*sale
*save, savings
   sensibly priced
*take advantage of...
   thrift, thrifty
   under...
*value, valuable
   well worth
   win, winner, winning
   your hard earned dollars

RELIGION

"**Religion**" is used here as a category of some human need or desire, a "good thing" already wanted or desired by people; ads often *simply associate* their product or service with "**religion**" words and images, thus *suggesting* or *implying* an "added value" to the buyer. In some situations, with some audiences, the common human desire for *certitude* (for support, reassurance, guidance, direction, approval) is related to this category of "religion."

In a free society, with diverse beliefs and practices, persuaders are aware that religion is a very sensitive issue: at best, a transcendent experience, involving reverence, worship, and altruism; at worst, a tool to exploit others, an opiate to drug others. Although association with religion is very common in *political persuasion* (the God-on-Our-Side theme; the linking of opponents with the devil, etc.), such heavy-handed association is *not common* in commercial advertising using *national* mass media in the USA; but, there's a great deal of such linking at the *local* level (church bulletins, religious radio programs, etc.) used to inform *specific* target audiences that certain products or sponsors are *"one of ours."* (Conversely, at times, that certain others should be boycotted.)

"**Religion**" words and images (including things *suggested indirectly* by backgrounds, context, music, sounds, metaphors, analogies, examples, and dramatized stories) are often clustered with other categories of human **needs and desires,** such as *nation, family,* and *generosity;* and often with words stressing **intrinsic** qualities such as *superiority, stability* of such **products and services** as some *books, LPs,* some *travel* (pilgrimages), *weddings,* etc.

SCARE AND SELL: "attack words" intensify the opposite, undesirable aspects: the lack of religious values; *sinful, ungodly, profane, blasphemous, impious, sacriligious,* etc.

RELIGION

KEY WORDS

blessed
charitable
charity
dedicated
devout
faith
faithful
fervent
hallowed
holy
honorable
just
piety
pious
pure
right
reverend
righteous
sacred
saintly
truth
virtuous
worship
zeal

SCIENCE

"Science" is used here as a category of some human need or desire, a "good thing" already wanted or desired by people; ads often *simply associate* their product or service with **"science"** words and images, thus *suggesting* or *implying* an "added value" to the buyer. In some situations, with some audiences, the common human desire for *certitude* (for support, reassurance, guidance, direction, approval) is related to this category of "science."

In a modern society, some say that science has replaced religion in the sense that some people have an almost-worshipful attitude toward scientific authority and technological progress which seems to promise cures, solutions, and a better life. Associating things with science and technology can also create the sense (or the illusion) of accuracy, certitude, and truth. Non-verbal images suggesting scientific authority are very common (labs, microscopes, white-coated doctors, complex machinery, computers, print-outs, synthesizer music, etc.) as is the use of *jargon* and *shop talk* from many scientific and technical areas (including psychology, computers, space technology). Together with scientific-sounding words using *Latin prefixes* and *suffixes* (mega-, mini-, micro-, hyper-, -ics, -ite, -ate), *abbreviations* and *acronyms* (DX7, Formula R2D, PEPSICO, EXXON), *numerical* and *statistical data,* there is a widespread use of science to lend prestige to many products and services.

"Science" words and images (including things *suggested indirectly* by backgrounds, context, music, sounds, metaphors, analogies, examples, and dramatized stories) are often clustered with other categories of human **needs and desires,** such as *health,* and *safety;* and often with words stressing **intrinsic** qualities such as *superiority, efficiency, reliability, practicality* of such **products and services** as: *medicines, drugs, cigarettes* (filters), *cars, machinery, appliances, "body work"* (diets, etc.).

SCARE AND SELL: "attack words" intensify the opposite, undesirable aspects: the lack of scientific values; *superstitions, ignorant, unskilled, illogical, unsubstantiated, inaccurate,* etc.

SCIENCE KEY WORDS

analyst
bionic
clinically tested
computer
documentation
electronics
experiment
laboratory
mechanics
medically proven
*research
*scientific
scientists
space age technology
state of the art
studies
technical
technicians
technology

BEST PEOPLE

"**Best people**" is used here as a category of some human or need desire, a "good thing" already wanted or desired by people; ads often *simply associate* their product or service with "**best people**" words and images, thus *suggesting* or *implying* an "added value" to the buyer. In some situations, with some audiences, the common human desire for *certitude* (for support, reassurance, guidance, direction, approval) is related to this category of an "elite."

Every era, every culture, every group has its own elite, people who are *leaders,* who are admired and esteemed by others: e.g., movie stars, millionaires, athletes, artists, popular singers, journalists, TV reporters, the "jet set," "high society," celebrities, etc. Sometimes this aristocracy is due to *wealth, birth* ("being in the right family"), or *beauty:* every group has its "beautiful people." Sometimes it's a "natural aristocracy" based on *virtue* or *talent,* the personality and achievements of a person rather than any unearned gifts. Yet, regardless of the source or basis, every group will have those esteemed leaders, heroes or experts, who lend authority, certitude, or prestige to that which is associated with them.

"**Best people**" words and images (including things *suggested indirectly* by backgrounds, context, music, sounds, metaphors, analogies, examples, and dramatized stories) are often clustered with other categories of human **needs and desires,** such as *groups, esteem,* and *creativity;* and often with words stressing **intrinsic** qualities such as *superiority, beauty,* and *scarcity* of such **products and services** as some *liquors, "body work,"* some *cosmetics, clothes,* some *cars, sporting goods, cameras, stereos,* some *entertainment, travel,* some *military* (e.g. Marines), some *colleges* and *job ads, homes, furniture,* some *retail stores, banks, credit cards,* etc.

SCARE AND SELL: "attack words" intensify the opposite, undesirable aspects: the lack of prestige; *commonplace, mediocre, second-rate, run-of-the mill,* etc.

BEST PEOPLE

KEY WORDS

aristocratic
award-winning
beautiful people
celebrated
celebrity
champion
cosmopolitan
elegant
elite
eminent
esteemed
exclusive
expert
expertise
famed
*famous
fashionable
illustrious
important
leaders
leadership
noted
noteworthy
prestige
prestigious
profession
professional
renowned
significant
society
urbane
win
winners

MOST PEOPLE

"**Most people**" is used here as a category of some human or need desire, a "good thing" *already* wanted or desired by people; ads often *simply associate* their product or service with "**most people**" words and images, thus *suggesting* or *implying* an "added value" to the buyer. In some situations, with some audiences, the common human desire for *certitude* (for support, reassurance, guidance, direction, approval) is related to this category of "popularity."

Often called the *"bandwagon"* appeal (an old-time metaphor of crowds jumping aboard the bandwagon of winning politicians), this category emphasizes the idea of *large numbers,* of doing or being like, what *"most people"* would approve. Such popularity appeals may be strongest in democratic societies which place high value on *majority* rule, and perhaps most intense in modern America, which Riesman has described as being "other-directed," that is, very concerned with the opinions and approval of other people (rather than "inner-directed" or "tradition-directed"). Such *peer-pressure,* (or "being popular," "one of the guys") is seen throughout society, but especially in persuasion directed at gathered groups (rallies, parades, demonstrations) or relying upon the authority, prestige, or "certitude" conferred by large numbers of people: "everyone's doing it." Today, it's very common to cite *polls:* (e.g. Harris poll, Nielsen ratings, Arbitron ratings, various "straw polls").

"**Most people**" words and images (including things *suggested indirectly* by backgrounds, context, music, sounds, metaphors, analogies, examples, and dramatized stories) are often clustered with other categories of human **needs and desires,** such as *average people, groups,* and *esteem;* and often with words stressing **intrinsic** qualities such as *superiority, efficiency, guantity, reliability, utility, simplicity* of such **products and services** as *foods, drink, beer, cigarettes, medicines, "body work," cosmetics, clothes,* (fads, fashions), some *cars, sporting goods, LP records, books, entertainments, cleaning aids,* some *military, colleges,* etc.

SCARE AND SELL: "attack words" intensify the opposite, undesirable aspects: the lack of popularity; *unpopular, unwanted, unliked, unknown,* etc.

MOST PEOPLE   KEY WORDS

        beloved by all
        best selling
        common agreement
        commonly
        consensus
        entire
        everyone
       *favorite
        general
        generally accepted
        majority
        more people
        most people
       *popular
        popularity
        prevailing
        total
        universally
        well beloved
        well liked
        widespread

AVERAGE PEOPLE

"**Average people**" is used here as a category of some human need or desire, a "good thing" *already* wanted or desired by people; ads often *simply associate* their product or service with "**average people**" words and images, thus *suggesting* or *implying* on "added value" to the buyer. In some situations, with some audiences, the common human desire for *certitude* (for support, reassurance, guidance, direction, approval) is related to this category of such "normality."

Often called the "plain folks" appeal, this category stresses the concept of "normality" or "typicality." Many people *see themselves* as being "typical," "normal," or "average." Thus, they would have empathy with, and be reassured by support or statements (testimonials, endorsements) made by *other* "normal" people. Sometimes the "average person" is personified abstractly (e.g., in America, *John Doe* or *John Q. Public;* in Russia, *Ivan Ivanovich;* in China, *Chang San);* sometimes a real person achieves fame as a "plain folk": Sgt. York (WW1), Audie Murphy (WW2), Billy Carter. This is related also to the "underdog" fantasy of the unknown person doing something heroic, being worthwhile: the benchwarmer winning the game, the understudy's debut in opera, the "ugly duckling" making good. "Plain folks" can be suggested by man-in-the-street interviews, "snapshot" pictures, *cinema-verite* movies (handheld camera, grainy film), "Plain" models, use of folk sayings, adages, maxims, folklore, etc.

"**Average people**" words and images (including things *suggested indirectly* by backgrounds, context, music, sounds, metaphors, analogies, examples, and dramatized stories) are often clustered with other categories of human **needs and desires,** such as *most people, neighborhood, groups;* and often with words stressing **intrinsic** qualities such as *superiority, efficiency, quantity, reliability, utility, simplicity* of such **products and services** as *soft drinks, beer, cigarettes, candy, snacks, foods, cosmetics, medicines, cars, LPs, books, entertainments, furniture, appliances, cleaning aids,* etc.

SCARE AND SELL: "attack words" intensify the opposite, undesirable aspects: the lack of being "typical" or "plain"; *snob, snobbish, uppity, arrogant, strange, odd, oddball,* etc.

AVERAGE PEOPLE

KEY WORDS

average
common
common sense
customary
down home
familiar
folk
folksy
genuine
horse-sense
hospitality
main stream
moderate
moderation
normal
ordinary
plain folks
rank and file
regular
salt-of-the-earth
simple
sincere
typical
usual

NEIGHBORHOOD

"**Neighborhood**" is used here as a category of some human need or desire, a "good thing" *already* wanted or desired by people; ads often *simply associate* their product or service with "**neighborhood**" words and images, thus *suggesting* or *implying* an "added value" to the buyer.

People love the familiar, the known, the close; one of our strongest ties to *space* and *territory* is the feeling we have for the specific region we consider our "neighborhood" or "home." Hometown pride is common ("Support your hometown merchants... Shop in your neighborhood... Local boy makes good"), but not limited to rural, small towns; all major cities have groups organized to promote civic pride, business, and tourism (via festivals, parades, songs, slogans, symbols, souvenirs, etc.). While some may criticize this as provincialism, such civic pride is also the basis for much of what we treasure: museums, libraries, the arts. The history of civilization is the history of the city.

In addition to our own hometown, some areas (Palm Beach, Newport, Malibu) also have desirable qualities, such as natural beauty, wealth or status of residents, which make the region have favorable associations. Ads often use such sites as backgrounds or in product names.

"**Neighborhood**" words and images (including things *suggested indirectly* by backgrounds, context, music, sounds, metaphors, analogies, examples, and dramatized stories) are often clustered with other categories of human **needs and desires,** such as *average people, groups, surroundings, nature, family;* and often with words stressing **intrinsic** qualities such as *superiority, beauty, quantity, stability* of such **products and services** as *beer* (local brands), *entertainments, college ads, homes* and *land, home repairs, local retail stores, funeral homes, banks, local radio* and *newspapers,* etc.

SCARE AND SELL: "attack words" intensify the opposite, undesirable aspects: the lack of regional ties; *stranger, outsider, intruder, newcomer, trespasser,* etc.

NEIGHBORHOOD

KEY WORDS

belong
belonging
civic
close
community
downtown
friendly
grassroots
hometown
local
nearby
neighbor
neighborhood
neighborly
region
regional

NATION

"**Nation**" is used here as a category of some human need or desire, a "good thing" *already* wanted or desired by people; ads often *simply associate* their product or service with "**nation**" words and images, thus *suggesting* or *implying* an "added value" to the buyer.

When modern nationalism emerged in Europe, groups put more emphasis on the artificial political boundaries created to divide the land. Boundaries have often changed since then, but the idea of nationalism has continued. Sometimes nationalism is linked to *religion,* especially in "holy wars" against the foreign "devils." Nationalism is often linked with *politics* and *economics:* capitalist countries idealize *"free enterprise"* ((downplaying corporate corruption, price-fixing, bribery, etc.); socialist countries idealize *"cooperation"* (downplaying government coercion, corruption, priviliged classes, etc.). Nations use symbols (flags, colors), songs (anthems, marches, slogans, etc.) to indoctrinate citizens. This is most intense during war or crisis when external enemies can be attacked, and citizens are pressured to prove their patriotism. *"Flag-waving"* in ads — linking the product or policy with patriotic appeals — is common, especially when domestic companies have foreign competition: e.g., "Keep America *free* from *dependence* on *foreign* oil."

"**Nation**" words and images (including things *suggested indirectly* by backgrounds, context, music, sounds, metaphors, analogies, examples, and dramatized stories) are often clustered with other categories of human **needs and desires,** such as *religion, average people, neighborhood, family, generosity;* and often with words stressing **intrinsic** qualities such as *superiority, quantity, stability,* and *beauty* of such **products and services** as *cars* and *manufactured goods,* ("Buy American!), *travel* ("See America First"), *military recruiting, U.S. Savings Bonds, corporate capitalism* ("American Way of Life"), etc.

SCARE AND SELL: "attack words" intensify the opposite, undesirable aspects: the lack of national ties; *traitor, disloyal, unAmerican, alien, foreign,* etc.

NATION KEY WORDS

allegiance
citizen
citizenship
country
father land
free
freedom
homeland
honor
independence
land
liberty
loyal
loyalty
national
patriot
patriotic
serve
service
sovereignity

in common phrasings (USA):
American dream
American heritage
American system
American way of life

in ads:
"Sears, where America shops"
"America is turning 7 Up"
"America spells cheese, K-R-A-F-T"
"See the USA in your Chevrolet"

NATURE

"**Nature**" is used here as a category of some human need or desire, a "good thing" *already* wanted or desired by people; ads often *simply associate* their product or service with "**nature**" words and images, thus *suggesting* or *implying* an "added value" to the buyer.

In the widest sense of "space" or "territory," people have a need to relate to *nature,* to the whole universe. The earth *is* beautiful and delightful to our senses: art and writings of all cultures indicate that people respond to the beauty of the oceans, the mountains, dense forests, open plains, autumn leaves, spring flowers, sunsets, rainbows, starry nights, snowfall, surf, and the animals which share life with us. People often romanticize nature with dreams of a tranquil pastoral scene, a pleasant Arcadia, a Garden of Eden paradise (downplaying the "bad" realities: storms, wild animals, "Nature red in fang and claw").

"**Nature**" words and images (including things *suggested indirectly* by backgrounds, context, music, sounds, metaphors, analogies, examples, and dramatized stories) are often clustered with other categories of human **needs and desires,** such as *health, food, nation, neighborhood, surroundings,* and often with words stressing **intrinsic** qualities such as *superiority, beauty, stability* of such **products and services** as *beer, cigarettes,* some *foods,* some *cereals,* some *medicines, cosmetics, travel,* some *homes* and *land,* etc.

SCARE AND SELL: "attack words" intensify the opposite, undesirable aspects: the lack of suitable natural environment; *unnatural, polluted, pollution; artificial, plastic,* (urban and technical concepts), etc.

NATURE　　　　　　　　　　　　　KEY WORDS

animals
beach
camping
earth
farm
field
fishing
forests
hikes
idyllic
lake
mountains
nature
*natural
ocean
open spaces
organic
outdoors
pastoral
picnics
plains
praries
rainbow
sea
shore
sky
streams
sunny
sunset
sunshine
wild
wilderness
wildlife
woods
woodsy

INTIMACY

"**Intimacy**" is used here as a category of some human need or desire, a "good thing" *already* wanted or desired by people; ads often *simply associate* their product or service with "**intimacy**" words and images, thus *suggesting* or *implying* an "added value" to the buyer.

A close, intimate relationship with another person is an important human desire. We seek to avoid loneliness and isolation; we seek a genuine love, without fear of rejection. Frequently, such ideal intimacy is linked with the ideals of marriage or of sexual partners, but not all marriages or sexual relationships are so intimate. Perhaps the idea of a "very close friend" might be closer to this ideal of intimacy which can be within a marriage or a sexual relationship, but may also occur elsewhere. Generally speaking, true intimacy is rare in any human situation. But the words which *promise* intimacy, or create an illusion of intimate behavior, are common in advertising because they touch on such deep human desire.

"**Intimacy**" words and images (including things *suggested indirectly* by backgrounds, context, music, sounds, metaphors, analogies, examples, and dramatized stories) are often clustered with other categories of human **needs and desires,** such as *activity, sex, family, groups, generosity;* and often with words stressing **intrinsic** qualities such as *superiority, beauty, scarcity,* and *stability* of such **products and services** as *cosmetics, "body work," clothes, wedding ads,* etc.

SCARE AND SELL: "attack words" intensify the opposite, undesirable aspects: the lack of intimacy; *unloved, unwanted, misunderstood, hate, abandoned, rejected, lonely,* etc.

INTIMACY　　　　　　　　　　KEY WORDS

affinity
attach
attract
attraction
beloved
bond
care
caring
close
closeness
commitment
considerate
couples
dear
desire
darling
embrace
feelings
friend
friendly
heartfelt
heartwarming
intimacy
intimate
love
lover
loving
partners
meaningful
personal
personalized
share
sharing
sweet
sweetheart
tender
tenderness
touch
touching
thoughtful
trust
trusting
understand
understanding

FAMILY

"**Family**" is used here as a category of some human need or desire, a "good thing" *already* wanted or desired by people; ads often *simply associate* their product or service with "**family**" words and images, thus *suggesting* or *implying* an "added value" to the buyer.

Although the "Mom and Apple Pie" stereotype of domestic pleasures is an exaggeration, it does touch on some of the most important human relationships of *love* and *bonding, nurturing* and *caring* within the family. The "public image" of family life is highly idealized: happy, cooperative people with solvable problems. But many real families have more difficult problems: child abuse, neglect, debts, divorce, hostility, neurotic behaviors, etc. Thus, when we see the "ideal" family in ads and on TV, we envy the illusion, desire the dream. Factory-made, mass-produced foods often seek to be associated with "home-made" virtues. Many other products also promise benefits *both* for *the buyer* (in role of provider and protector) and for *the family:* "you'll be a better parent, if you buy this for the family."

"**Family**" words and images (including things *suggested indirectly* by backgrounds, context, music, sounds, metaphors, analogies, examples, and dramatized stories) are often clustered with other categories of human **needs and desires,** such as *food, health, security, religion, nation, neighborhood, intimacy, generosity;* and often with words stressing **intrinsic** qualities such as *superiority, quantity, stability, reliability, safety, utility,* and *simplicity* of such **products and services** as *foods, medicines, clothes,* some *cars, cameras* (snapshots, home movies), some *entertainments, homes, home repairs, furniture, insurance, baby care, toys,* etc.

SCARE AND SELL: "attack words" intensify the opposite, undesirable aspects: the lack of family bonds; *disowned, unwanted, unloved, rejected, unappreciative, uncaring, irresponsible,* etc.

FAMILY   **KEY WORDS**

care
caring
domestic
domestic bliss
down home
family
family style
fireside
hearth
home
home grown
home maker
home made
home spun
hospitality
kitchen
nurture
protect
responsibility
serenity
sharing
togetherness
tranquil

Family relationship names:
Mother, Mom, Ma
Father, Pop, Pa
child, children, kids, baby
son, daughter
Grandma, Gram, Grannie, Nana
Grandfather, Grandpa, Gramps
Aunt, Auntie, Uncle, Sissie

Nicknames, pet names (Skipper, Kit)
Diminutives (Jimmy, Davy, Lizzie)

GROUPS

"**Groups**" is used here as a category of some human need or desire, a "good thing" *already* wanted or desired by people; ads often *simply associate* their product or service with "**Group**" words and images, thus *suggesting* or *implying* an "added value" to the buyer.

People are *social* animals. We want to *belong*. We often *identify ourselves* as being members of a certain group. People differ in the degree of identification they have with groups. Often, people with low self-esteem can get feelings of self-worth by emphasizing affiliation with a group, by being dedicated to a team, a group or a "cause." *Natural* groups are those we belong to, without choice (race, sex, age, background, being handicapped or gifted); *Choice* groups are our voluntary associations: Scouts, Little League, social clubs, colleges, athletic teams, political parties, religions, cults, occupation, hobbies, etc. We *choose* to do certain things in life; we choose to identify ourselves as being part of certain groups, often ignoring or downplaying our membership in other categories.

"**Group**" words and images (including things *suggested indirectly* by backgrounds, context, music, sounds, metaphors, analogies, examples, and dramatized stories) are often clustered with other categories of human **needs and desires,** such as *esteem, best people, average people, intimacy, neighborhood, religion;* and often with words stressing **intrinsic** qualities such as *superiority, stability* of such **products and services** as *soft drinks, beer, cosmetics, clothes,* some *cars, sporting goods, entertainments, military recruiting ads, colleges,* etc.

SCARE AND SELL: "attack words" intensify the opposite, undesirable aspects: the lack of group bonds; *outcast, rejected, excluded, disrupter, unfriendly, separate, detached, lonely,* etc.

GROUPS

KEY WORDS

associate
association
belong
belonging
buddies
combine
common
companion
companionship
congenial
convivial
cooperate
cooperative
cordial
fellowship
friend
friendly
friendship
group
gregarious
guest
harmonious
harmony
help
helping
hospitable
hospitality
host
invitation
invite
introduce
involved
like
loyal
loyalty
mutual
outgoing
pals
sociable
social
team spirit
teamwork
together
united
unified

ESTEEM

"**Esteem**" is used here as a category of some human need or desire, a "good thing" *already* wanted or desired by people; ads often *simply associate* their product or service with "**esteem**" words and images, thus *suggesting* or *implying* an "added value" to the buyer.

Esteem is a social need: we seek to be recognized and valued by others. Both dominance and submission are involved in a social order. *Aggressive* behaviors are encouraged by emphasis on *esteem,* leadership, winning, competition, dominance. *(Submissive* behaviors are encouraged by emphasis on *belonging,* joining, fitting in, being accepted, altruism, loyalty to the group, teamwork, generosity, etc.) In a society which is "open," not rigidly ordered, ads often stress *upward mobility* (improve, get better); products promise a raising of social status. Seeking after *unobtainable* goals can cause serious dissatisfaction; fortunately, we have the option of seeking esteem in *many* different groups or categories, or seeking other needs or desires in the place of positional goals.

"**Esteem**" words and images (including things *suggested indirectly* by backgrounds, context, music, sounds, metaphors, analogies, examples, and dramatized stories) are often clustered with other categories of human **needs and desires,** such as *activity, generosity, best people, groups,* and often with words stressing **intrinsic** qualities such as *superiority, beauty, scarcity, stability, reliability* of such **products and services** as *"body work,"* cosmetics, clothes, cars, stereos, books, entertainments, travel, military, college, and *job ads, wedding ads, homes, furniture,* etc.

SCARE AND SELL: "attack words" intensify the opposite, undesirable aspects: the lack of esteem; *unknown, overlooked, nobody, insignificant, loser; hated, scorned, detested, despised, infamous,* etc.

ESTEEM KEY WORDS

acclaim
acclaimed
admire
admired
appreciated
approval
approved
champion
cherished
chief
distinction
dominant
*expert
expertise
famous
foremost
hero, heroic
honor
honored
*important
influential
leader
leadership
leading
master
mastery
noted
noteworthy
noticeable
praise
praised
prestige
prestigious
prized
prominent
recognized
regarded
respect
respected
revered
significant
success
*successful
valued
win, winner

PLAY

'**Play**" is used here as a category of some human need or desire, a "good thing" *already* wanted or desired by people; ads often *simply associate* their product or service with "**play**" words and images, thus *suggesting* or *implying* an "added value" to the buyer.

Playful behaviors can be observed in several species of higher animals, but human play is distinctive for its *wide diversity* and relatively great *amount of time* devoted to such non-utilitarian ends. We spend a lot of time and effort in fun and games. This varies with the affluence of the society and the individuals; but even in some rather grim situations, people take "time out" or "take a break" to play, to restore or refresh themselves, to divert their attention often from harsh or painful necessities. Play activities can range from the solitary imagination to elaborate commercial playgrounds (e.g., Disney World). Perhaps play is more "useful" than it first appears: *activity* is beneficial to the healthy well-being of the body, *curiosity* is stimulating to the mind. Play can be a release of tensions or a *rehearsing of roles* or modeling behavior, often a *bonding* of people in group activity.

"**Play**" words and images (including things *suggested indirectly* by backgrounds, context, music, sounds, metaphors, analogies, examples, and dramatized stories) are often clustered with other categories of human **needs and desires,** such as *activity, groups, curiosity;* and often with words stressing **intrinsic** qualities such as *superiority* and *novelty* of such **products and services** as *"body work"* (esp. exercise), *cars, cycles, sporting goods, stereos, LPs, books, entertainments, travel* (vacations), *toys,* etc.

SCARE AND SELL: "attack words" intensify the opposite, undesirable aspects: the lack of a playful attitude; *dull, solemn, sad, austere, grave,* etc.

PLAY
KEY WORDS

amuse
amusement
amusing
celebrate
celebration
cheerful
diversion
*enjoy
enjoyment
entertain
entertainment
fun
funny
glad
happy
happiness
hilarious
jolly
joy
joyful
merry
party
play
playful
pleasant
pleasing
pleasure
recreate
recreation
refresh
refreshing

GENEROSITY

"**Generosity**" is used here as a category of some human need or desire, a "good thing" *already* wanted or desired by people; ads often *simply associate* their product or service with "**generosity**" words and images, thus *suggesting* or *implying* an "added value" to the buyer.

Giving away runs contrary to the human desire to possess, but such generosity is often considered a higher human virtue. At best, gifts are symbolic expressions of *love, altruism, bonding* in the social order. However, not all gifts are given so freely or without some kind of strings attached.*Reciprocity (quid pro quo,* "tit for tat") gifts are those which expect some kind of return favor, perhaps some kind of gratitude, thanks, or approval. *Guilt* is another reason for giving, an attempt to "make up" or "pay back" for an offense or an omission. Such giving involves a sense of debt, duty, or obligation. Ads stress the *gratitude* of the receivers and the *reward* for the givers: "She'll be *pleased, delighted, grateful...* She'll *remember, treasure, appreciate* your *thoughtfulness, concern,* etc." In our society, special gift-giving days include Christmas, birthdays, Mother's Day, Valentines Day, weddings, anniversaries, graduations, religious days. Religions and nations also ask people *to give to* or *to serve,* their Faith, Church, Country, Team, etc. To die for one's Faith or Country is often highly priased by the institutions involved.

"**Generosity**" words and images (including things *suggested indirectly* by backgrounds, context, music, sounds, metaphors, analogies, examples, and dramatized stories) are often clustered with other categories of human **needs and desires,** such as *religion, nation, intimacy, family, esteem;* and often with words stressing **intrinsic** qualities such as *superiority, beauty, scarcity* of such **product and services** as expensive *liquor,* some *cosmetics* (perfume), *clothes, cars, entertainments, wedding ads, appliances, baby care, toys,* etc.

SCARE AND SELL: "attack words" intensify the opposite, undesirable aspects: the *lack of generosity; stingy, cheap, miserly, selfish, egocentric, self-centered,* etc.

GENEROSITY

KEY WORDS

aid
altruistic
appreciate
appreciated
beloved
benevolent
care
caring
charitable
charity
cherish
cherished
delight
delighted
generous
gift
give
gratitude
grateful
help
helping
keepsake
loved ones
please
pleased
remember
reward
serve
service
share
sharing
treasure
treasured
treat

CURIOSITY

"**Curiosity**" is used here as a category of some human need or desire, a "good thing" *already* wanted or desired by people; ads often *simply associate* their product or service with "**curiosity**" words and images, thus *suggesting* or *implying* an "added value" to the buyer.

People want to know, to find out about the unknown. Such curiosity (very important for the species) ranges from *scientific investigation* to *gossip:* we are interested in what is going on around us, what happened in the past, what will happen in the future. Educational systems (such as schools, libraries, newspapers, TV) help keep us informed, stimulate our intellect, appeal to our curiosity, reduce our boredom when we are not stimulated enough. People are curious about the *secrets of others,* the *unknown* or *hidden* aspects of family, friends, famous celebrities (eavesdropping, prying into others' affairs, voyeurism, etc.), about the *unusual,* the *atypical, exotic,* the *oddity,* the *far away;* about the future: *prophecy predictions, omens, superstitions, astrology.*

"**Curiosity**" words and images (including things *suggested indirectly* by backgrounds, context, music, sounds, metaphors, analogies, examples, and dramatized stories) are often clustered with other categories of human **needs and desires,** such as *activity, play, science;* and often with words stressing **intrinsic** qualities such as *superiority* and *novelty* of such **products and services** as *books, magazines, newspapers, colleges,* some *entertainments, TV, travel,* etc.

SCARE AND SELL: "attack words" intensify the opposite, undesirable aspects: the lack of curiosity; *uninterested, boring, dull, shallow, apathetic,* etc.

CURIOSITY KEY WORDS

adventure
"backstage"
"behind the scenes"
clever
discover
discovery
educational
engaging
engrossing
explore
exploration
expose
fascinating
find out
inform
informative
ingenious
inquisitive
"inside story"
intelligent
interesting
intriguing
investigate
investigation
learn
learning
news
newsworthy
reveal
revelation
secret
uncover
witty

CREATIVITY

'Creativity'' is used here as a category of some human need or desire, a "good thing" *already* wanted or desired by people; ads often *simply associate* their product or service with **"creativity"** words and images, thus *suggesting* or *implying* an "added value" to the buyer.

While only a few (e.g., Beethoven, Edison) are usually known as a "creative genius," millions of people have created new things. "Creativity" isn't limited to a few people or to certain areas: the essence of creativity is *making something new.* People need to feel that their work is important, significant, useful or unique; we have a desire for the kind of "living on" or "immortality" which we gain when we create new things. Many ads, however, tend to separate "creativity" from our normal work life, and to restrict it to words and images associated with the fine arts, or to pre-packaged entertainments (e.g., paint-by-number sets) which sell the *illusion* of creativity.

"Creativity" words and images (including things *suggested indirectly* by backgrounds, context, music, sounds, metaphors, analogies, examples, and dramatized stories) are often clustered with other categories of human **needs and desires,** such as *best people, esteem,* and *completion;* and often with words stressing **intrinsic** qualities such as *superiority, scarcity,* and *novelty* of such **products and services** as *cameras, books, LP records,* some *entertainment,* some *college ads,* some *job ads,* etc.

SCARE AND SELL: "attack words" intensify the opposite, undesirable aspects: the lack of creativity' *unimaginative, untalented, uncreative, unoriginal, imitative, lazy,* etc.

CREATIVITY

KEY WORDS

architect
artist
artistic
author
avant-garde
build
builder
composer
composition
craft
craftsmanship
create
creative
creativity
creator
culture
cultural
design
do
dramatic
energy
imagine
imagination
invent
inventor
make
maker
original
originality
plan
skill
talent
talented
work

COMPLETION

"**Completion**" is used here as a category of some human need or desire, a "good thing" *already* wanted or desired by people; ads often *simply associate* their product or service with "**completion**" words and images, thus *suggesting* or *implying an "added value" to the buyer.*

People have always been workers, builders, makers, creators, and problem-solvers. One of the joys we have is that of *"closure,"* of completion, of getting a job done, a problem solved. When something is undone, incomplete, people often feel a strong desire to close, to reach a conclusion, to achieve a goal. "Success" in human achievements can vary widely in kind and degree, from a national effort (a space mission) to individual efforts (school graduation) or even entertainments (solving puzzles, riddles, mysteries). Two common kinds of ads relate to completing a *set* or a *sequence:* (1) ads for "collections" (coins, books, plates) expect *many to start* and *some to complete;* also, some products are designed to encourage the purchase of *"extras,"* and accessories; (2) ads for "improvement" items (dance, diet, job) relate to an endless cycle of "getting better." *Serialization* (stories, movies, LPs) is related to our desire to continue and complete a sequence.

"**Completion**" words and images (including things *suggested indirectly* by backgrounds, context, music, sounds, metaphors, analogies, examples, and dramatized stories) are often clustered with other categories of human **needs and desires,** such as *activity, esteem,* and *creativity;* and often with words stressing **intrinsic** qualities such as *superiority, efficiency, rapidity, simplicity* of such **products and services** as *"body work," cars, cameras, stereos, appliances,* (extras, accessories); *LP records* (collections): *college ads, job ads* (improvements), etc.

SCARE AND SELL: "attack words" intensify the opposite, undesirable aspects: the lack of completion; *incomplete, frustrated, abandoned, quitter, failure,* etc.

COMPLETION

KEY WORDS

achieve
*achievement
accomplish
*accomplishment
climax
close
closure
collect
*collection
complete
completion
composure
conclude
conclusion
content
contentment
end
finish
fulfill
fulfillment
full, fullness
get it done
goal
graduate
graduation
harmony
harmonious
mature
maturity
order
ordered
perform
performance
perfect
perfection
reach
ripe, ripeness
*satisfaction
satisfy
solve
solution
succeed
*success
successful
synthesis
whole

SOME STANDARD PHRASING

Some standard phrasing is found in many ads: asserting that a benefit *exists,* that the buyer (or other) *desires* it, and that it produces the desired effect *(satisfaction);* these are often phrased as *direct commands,* or in variations such as *negatives* and *rhetorical questions.*

Actual use of these standard phrases varies with the situation. Direct commands, for example, as if they were orders or imperatives coming from a parent figure or an authority figure, are part of the "hard sell." As such, they may be less common on television than in person-to-person selling when the persuader senses that the buyer will tolerate or submit to it. However, most people *in unfamiliar situations* (travel, car repairs, etc.) will accept very strong directives offered as tips, advice, or guides.

ASSERTING A BENEFIT:
Save (time, money, effort, etc.)...
Get (a specific benefit)...
Improve... Be *more...* Be *better...*
Enjoy...
Stop... Solve... Prevent... Avoid... (a problem)

DIRECTIVES, DIRECT COMMANDS:
You *need...*
You *should* get...
You *must* have...
You *ought* to...
You *have* to...

VARIATIONS — NEGATIVES AND RHETORICAL QUESTIONS:
Don't be *disappointed...*
Don't *worry...*
Don't be *sorry...*
Need it? *Want* it?...
Wouldn't Mom be *pleased?...*
Shouldn't you *really* have?...
Avoid *disappointment...*
Don't you *deserve* it?...

ASSERTING DESIRE:
Just what you've always *wanted...*
Everything you *desire* in...
What you've always *hoped* for...
Just what you *expected* from...
Everything you've *dreamed* of...

ASSERTING SATISFACTION:
You'll *enjoy...*
You'll be *pleased...*
You'll be *happy...*
You'll *love...*
You'll *like...*
You'll be *satisfied...*

ASSERTING SATISFACTION AND DESIRE BY OTHERS: (Gifts)
Your family *needs...*
The kids will *love...*
Show them you *care...*
She'll be *pleased...*
He'll *enjoy...*
Delight your family...
Reward them with...
Your dog will *love...*

To re-cap: The main part of "the pitch" is concerned with benefits. As **benefit-seekers,** human behavior can be described in terms of **protection** (Keep the "good"), **acquisition** (Get the "good"), **relief** (Change the "bad"), and **prevention** (Avoid the "bad"). Advertisers, as **benefit-promisers,** direct their appeals to these by making certain **claims** and **promises:** Claims about **themselves** (as being competent, trustworthy, and benevolent — discussed in Chapter 3) and about the **intrinsic merits** of their products (superiority, quantity, beauty, efficiency, etc.); and promises that benefits result, either from their product, or suggesting some **"added values"** by associating their product with some human needs and wants (such as food, sex, security, belonging, esteem) already desired by the audience.

To Analyze an Ad, Ask these Key Questions:

- **Who is the target audience?** Are *you?* (If *not,* as part of an unintended audience, are you *uninterested* or *hostile* toward the ad?)

- **What is the primary motive of that audience's benefit-seeking?**

Use chart at right. ▶ Most ads are simple acquisition. Often motives co-exist, but one may be dominant.	To keep a "good" *(protection)*	To Get rid of a "bad" *(relief)*
	To get a "good" *(acquisition)*	To avoid a "bad" *(prevention)*

- **What kinds of product claims are emphasized?** (Such as *superiority, quantity, efficiency, beauty,* etc.) With what key words and images? Any *measurable* claims? Or are they *subjective opinions, generalized* praise words, *puffery?*

- **Are any "added values" implied or suggested?** Are there words or images which **associate** the product with some "good" already loved or desired by the intended audience? With such common human needs/wants/desires as food, activity, sex, esteem etc.

4

URGENCY-STRESSING

    Creating a sense of **urgency** is common in some, but not all, advertising. Some people distinguish between *"hard sell"* and *"soft sell"* advertising depending whether or not there is an urgency plea. Others use the term "hard sell" more broadly to suggest any kind of aggressive techniques, such as intimidating salespeople who brow-beat customers in person-to-person transactions.
    In this book, the five-part pattern of "the pitch" is presented as the *basic* pattern of advertising, even though many ads *do not use* an urgency plea (#4: "Hurry") or a specific call for action (#5: "Buy").

However, using this five-part pattern emphasizes that the ultimate purpose (the "bottom line") of advertising, even when it is not explicitly stated, is some kind of *response*. By trying to apply this full pattern, the more likely you are to notice when there are omissions, to distinguish between "command propaganda" and "conditioning propaganda," and to recognize the varieties of "conditioning propaganda," such as the "soft sell" and "image building" ads.

"Command propaganda," as used here, means persuasion attempts which seek an *immediate response* (NOW!). For example, "the pitch" is used here as the pattern of command propaganda in commercial advertising.

"Conditioning propaganda," as used here, means persuasion which seeks to mold public opinion, assumptions, beliefs, and attitudes on a long-term basis as the necessary climate or atmosphere for a *future response* (LATER!).

When the urgency appeal is used, whether in advertising or in political situations, it tends to stress the emotions rather than thoughtful contemplation. Although some urgency claims (such as, *real* emergencies, *actual* time limitations) are genuine, many are artificial. They are designed to rush us into action: to buy something, to do something, or to believe something, without adequate thought or critical judgment.

The urgency plea usually seeks to force an issue into a crisis, and to narrow the options to *two:* yes or no, stop or go. Although such a tactic probably forces some people to choose "no" (to decide against the persuader), it also forces a certain number to choose "yes." Logically, the urgency appeal seeks to create a *contradictory* relationship instead of a *contrary* relationship (in which other options are available); psychologically, such urgency seeks to increase our anxiety about losing a benefit.

Advertisers and politicians are not the only ones to use urgency please. Poets and lovers have traditionally urged their beloved ones to "seize the day": this *"carpe diem"* theme is common in poetry. Folk sayings, too, encourage us to "strike while the iron is hot" and that "fortune favors the bold." (Alas, folk sayings also tell us that "haste makes waste" and that "fools rush in where angels fear to tread.") No matter who uses the urgency appeal, there's a risk; persuaders are always concerned with the relative effectiveness, in different situations, of the relaxed "soft sell" or the urgent "hard sell."

URGENCY KEY WORDS

Act now...
Available only...
Beat the crowd...
Clearance...
Come in now...
Deadline...
Do it now...
Don't delay...
Don't miss out...
Don't wait...
Enter now...
Final close-out...
Going fast...
Going out of business...
Golden opportunity...
Hurry...
Last chance...
Limited offer...
Midnight Madness...
Never again...
No later than...
Now is the time...
Now or never...
Offer expires...
Opportunity knocks...
One day only...
One week only...
Once in a lifetime...
Only five left...
Only 7 shopping days left until Christmas...
Promptness bonus...
Prices going up...
Rush...
See it today...
Time running out...
Today only...
Weekend sale...

Urgency can be expressed in *common words* (hurry, now, last chance, etc.) or in *"crossroads" metaphors* (decision point, critical point, junction, now or never, either/or) or in *nonverbal cues* (quickening tempo in music, staccato sounds, ticking clocks, countdowns, or images of motion). Although basically related to *time,* urgency pleas are often clustered with concepts of *scarcity* (lack of quantity), and *availability* (chance, opportunity).

Some advertisers claim a kind of moral superiority because they use the "soft sell." Some retail stores, for example, pride themselves on non-aggressive sales clerks and low-key ads. But, there are many situations in which the "soft sell" simply is *more appropriate* and *more effective* than any pushy strategy. Sellers of expensive items (autos, homes, major appliances, etc.) often advertise, encouraging their audience to "shop around and compare prices." This is a safe strategy for using a "soft sell": most people do comparison shopping for these items anyway.

Many nationally advertised products of standard consumer items (foods, necessities, etc.) can use a "soft sell" effectively, depending on long-term *repetition.* Campbell's Soups, for example, have been encouraging soup for lunch for over fifty years; fifty years hence, they still will be. Coca-Cola has been giving us "good times" ads for nearly a century. Such advertising need not be strident, nor seek instant response. These corporations seek long-term and repeated use of their products, and reasonably expect that they will get a certain percentage of the total market.

Much of the advertising industry's bad reputation has been caused by the use of urgency techniques, by the "fast hustle" and the "hard sell" of unscrupulous fly-by-night operators. Although the urgency technique is "neutral" (can be used for good or bad purposes, genuine emergency or artificial scare, effectively or ineffectively), there are some common situations in which the urgency appeal, as part of the "hard sell," is likely to be used, in contrast with those situations in which a "soft sell" is conditioning the audience for a later response.

COMMON SITUATIONS FOR:

"HARD SELL"
(command, using urgency appeal)

"SOFT SELL"
(Conditioning, for later)

---

when PRODUCT is temporary:
limited or one-time use:

FADS, FASHIONS
ENTERTAINMENTS, MOVIES, LPS, TOYS
SEASONAL CLOTHING & EQUIPMENT
PERISHABLE FOODS

when PRODUCT has repeated use:

STANDARD FOODS
NON-FASHION CLOTHING

---

when SELLER is temporary:

DOOR-TO-DOOR SELLING
TELEPHONE SOLICITATIONS "boiler room"
FLY-BY-NIGHT OPERATIONS "one-shot"
CON GAMES ("pigeon drop")

when SELLER is permanent:

ESTABLSHED STORES

---

when BUYER is temporary, that is
in an unfamiliar *area* **or** *condition:*

TOURISTS, TRAVELERS
NEWCOMERS
INEXPERIENCED
IMMATURE

when BUYER is stabile and familiar:

RESIDENTS, IN OWN AREA
EXPERIENCED MATURE ADULTS

---

when geniune CRISIS exists:
an emergency, a time limit, deadline

PAIN, ILLNESS (buyer very vulnerable)
SALES (genuine close-outs, etc.)
ELECTIONS

when no time urgency exists:

HEALTH
BUSINESS AS USUAL

---

when GUARANTEE (RETURN OF GOODS,
REPRISAL), is missing:

UNKNOWN CORPORATIONS
"FRONTS"

when GUARANTEE is explicit or
implicit:

ESTABLISHED CORPORATIONS
NAME BRANDS

---

when SUPPLY EXCEEDS DEMAND:

SURPLUS SITUATIONS

when DEMAND EXCEEDS SUPPLY:

SHORTAGE SITUATIONS

"THE PITCH"
ATTENTION-GETTING   CONFIDENCE-BUILDING    DESIRE-STIMULATING

[Hi!]   [Trust me!]   [You need!]

URGENCY-STRESSING    RESPONSE-SEEKING

[Hurry!]   [Buy!]

Figure 3. **"THE PITCH,"** as used here, describes the basic pattern of **"command propaganda"** as seen in commercial advertising. This five-part pattern stresses the most common sequence, moving toward an explicit call for a specific action.

"SOFT SELL"
ATTENTION-GETTING   CONFIDENCE-BUILDING    DESIRE-STIMULATING

[Hi!]   [Trust me!]   [You need!]

Figure 4." As used here, the **"soft sell"** describes a pattern of **"conditioning propaganda"** as seen in commercial advertising, preparing the audience for a response *later.* There is *no* urgency plea. The response sought may be *implied,* rather than explicitly stated. Standard brands (e.g. Coca Cola, Campbell's Soups) may simply delete the urgency plea (they'll still be around next year) and imply a response. Often such advertisers compensate by *repetition* (in quantity, frequency, and long-term duration).

"IMAGE BUILDING"

ATTENTION-GETTING   CONFIDENCE-BUILDING

[face saying "Hi!"]   [face saying "Trust me!"]

Figure 5. **"Image building"** is used here to describe a pattern of **"conditioning propaganda"** which does *not* call (explicitly or implicitly) for a specific response. Closely related, or synonymous, to: "publicity," "public relations," "PR," "goodwill advertising," "corporate advertising," "institutional advertising." Often, there are *no consumer products* involved, such as in ads by IBM, Xerox, Cargil, U.S. Steel, Dow, Union Carbide, TRW, United Technologies. Often such ads are meant to make public "feel good" about large corporations: to create a favorable climate of public opinion; to reduce public demand for government regulations, taxes; to counter negative images of "monopolies," "middlemen," or "merchants of death."

To re-cap: Creating a sense of **urgency** is common in some, but not all, advertising. Much advertising is **command propaganda** seeking an *immediate* response, but some is **conditioning propaganda** preparing for a *future* response. Both the "soft sell" and "image building" are variations of such conditioning.

To Analyze an Ad, Ask these Key Questions:

- **Are there urgency-stressing techniques used?**

- **If so, with what words?** (e.g. Hurry, Rush, Offer Expires) **What nonverbals?**

- **If no urgency,** is this **"soft sell"** part of a repetitive, long-term ad campaign for a standard item?

5

RESPONSE-SEEKING

Response is the goal, the basic intent and the final purpose of "the pitch." Advertising, for example, is meant *to sell* a product; attention-getting may be the first important step of the process, but an *effective* ad, ultimately, must provoke a response. Some ads may be clever, witty, humorous, entertaining, informational, or educational: but if they don't achieve their intended goal, if they don't *sell* the product, they are not effective.

Certainly with "soft sell" or "image building" advertising, almost any pleasant, inoffensive ad could be justified or defended as achieving its vague or unmeasureable goal. But, much commercial advertising is command propaganda designed to sell specific products, at a specific cost-effectiveness, during a specific time. If this is not achieved, the persuader's job is to seek another approach.

Many ads may be praiseworthy for the high quality of the writing, the artwork or the acting; but the basic criteria for judging persuasion, *per se,* is *pragmatic:* does it work? Is it effective? Obviously, we also make *ethical* judgments about the morality of an ad, and *esthetic* judgments about the beauty; but these three aspects are separate and distinct, and often do not coincide. Many of the detergent commercials, for example, are sexist, trite, vulgar, and, unfortunately, very effective. This is one of the realities in our less-than-perfect world.

Making the response *easy* is one of the persuader's most important jobs. *Skilled persuaders know that it's not very useful to call for a difficult, complex, or impossible response.* Advertisers will seek a simple response, such as "buy" or the simple first step of a buying sequence: "Send for... Shop at... Go to... Mail... Call... See your dealer..." Advertisers are very concerned with removing obstacles, making it easy to respond.

"Impulse buying," for example, describes how this principle is applied in "point-of-purchase" advertising: the displays and merchandise set up in stores, usually right near the check-out counter where people wait in line. The merchandise is easily available, convenient to pick up and buy, and is usually linked with an urgency plea: *on sale, now!*

Removing obstacles to the response also includes the removal of *fears* which can be accomplished in the early part of the pitch: establishing confidence in the speakers and products — "Trust Me."

"Closing the sale" is the important part in person-to-person selling. Most people have participated in these transactions, in roles both of buyers and sellers. But some people are especially skilled in the art of closing a sale. In selling houses and cars, for example, some sellers are the "closers" who are best able to get the customer to say "yes" and to sign the contract. There's a whole range of nonverbal techniques of salesmanship available: making people feel obligated to buy, or embarrassed not to buy; filling out paperwork for the sale *as if* consent had already been given, ringing up the cash register, or asking about "extra" information ("What color do you want?"; "Will it be cash or charge?") *as if* consent had already been given. In person-to-person selling, the persuader can change tactics and can use different techniques if the buyer doesn't respond. But in advertising in the mass media, the persuader doesn't have the same kind of feedback. It's much *more difficult* to get response, but it's also much *more economical.* Therefore, advertisers have developed many ingenious ways by which individuals can make some kind of personal response to these messages broadcast to millions.

RESPONSE   **KEY WORDS**

Act now...
Buy...
Apply...
Call, toll free (800)...
Choose...
Come to...
Drink...
Eat...
Enclose your check...
Enjoy...
Experience...
Fill out and return...
Get...
Go to...
Join...
Mail this card...
Make your offer...
Obtain...
Order...
Pick up your phone...
Purchase...
Register...
See your local...
Select...
Send money order...
Send today...
Shop at...
Sign here...
Smoke...
Subscribe...
Taste...
Use...
Write...

MASS MEDIA RESPONSE

Direct mail advertising (known to its critics as "junk mail") developed some of the oldest and most successful response devices: C.O.D. mail delivery service, pre-paid Business Reply Envelopes, post cards, and variety of "blow-in" and/or "rip-out" cards inserted into magazines, and so on.

Coupons are especially popular as response-getters. Billions of "cents off" coupons are distributed every year by mail, newspapers, and magazines. Millions of people are coupon-clippers. Coupons are a very effective device to get response, especially for food products; not only do people buy the products, but also the sales campaign can be *measured* by counting the coded coupons redeemed.

Sweepstakes and contests are popular devices which frequently get good response of people buying the product or going to the store to pick up the entry blank. Federal anti-lottery laws prohibit sweepstakes which *require* a purchase; therefore to remain legal, sweepstakes must accept the "plain 3 x 5 card, etc." entry as equal to an entry which encloses the product's boxtop or wrapper. However, many people *feel* that they have a "better chance" if they send in the wrapper!

Yes/No Tokens, Stamps (to paste in boxes), checkmarks (to make), are all attempts by direct mail advertisers to get some kind of *active* response, to avoid having the advertisement being thrown away, unopened, as junk mail. (You can't persuade if no one's listening or watching!) When the *Reader's Digest,* for example, makes a major mailing to solicit subscribers, the magazine may send out more than 10 million pieces in one mailing, a very expensive operation. By experience, they know that a sweepstakes (a relatively minor expense) will increase, by a few percentage points, the number of people who will open and read their message, and also the number who will buy.

The telephone has become an important response device during the past generation. In the early days of radio, telephones were not a primary response device; but, during the 1950s, both television and the telephone network expanded and developed together. TV advertisers were quick to see the value of having people make an immediate response by phoning in an order. By the 1970s, the technique was much more sophisticated by offering a *free call,* using the (800) area-code system, and making a direct billing transaction if the customer had a Masterchage or Visa card number.

Future response devices, being tested now, will include the use of two-way cable systems (CATV), home computers or terminals, together with Electronic Funds Transfers (EFT). The electronic gadgets may vary, but the basic purpose is the same: **response.**

If you've ever thought that commercials were "the best thing on TV," you're not alone in your assessment. Many professional writers, directors, cinematographers, artists and scholars think so too. In his excellent analysis of the mythic qualities of TV commercials *(The Best Thing on TV,* Penguin, 1978) Jonathan Price begins by itemizing their virtues:

> — They're coldly calculated: Since a commercial is designed as part of a marketing strategy, its objectives are studiously worked out beforehand; compared to program writers, the creators of commercials are far more conscious of the impact they are making.
>
> — They're carefully written: Since every second costs more than two thousand dollars, crack writers sand every idea and plan every camera angle for maximum effect, making the authors of *60 Minutes* look like tourists casually writing home.
>
> — They're overdirected: Shooting one hundred feet of film for every one they use, commercial directors caress every detail until it glows: particularly on food, hair, and cars, the results are bravura...
>
> Culturally, commercials have trained our eye to accept fast cuts, dense and highly paced imagery, very brief scenes, connections that are implied but not spelled out — in brief, a new style of visual entertainment.
>
> Historically, we see commercials more often than the shows (the same spot may be run six to sixty times a season), and we recall them in more detail, often with more fondness...
>
> Financially, commercials represent the pinnacle of our popular culture's artistic expression. More money per second goes into their making, more cash flows from their impact, more business thinking goes into each word than in any movie, opera, stage play, painting, or videotape. If commercials are artful, then the art is objective, not subjective; capitalist, not rebellious; part of a social activity rather than a personal search for expression; more like a Roman road than a lyric poem. Their beauty is economic...
>
> Commercials are not all superb. But the best are lively, very American mini-dramas, tiny films, high-speed epics. Taken as a whole, commercials offer a rough catalogue of our consumer economy and a wild tour of our unconscious fantasies.

To re-cap: Response is the goal, the basic intent, and ultimate purpose of "the pitch." Persuaders will seek to make response easy, to limit options, and to use triggering words, simple directives telling us what to do. Mass media response devices include a variety of coupons, contests, blow-in cards, and (800) phone calls.

To Analyze an Ad, Ask these Key Questions:

- **Are there specific triggering words used?** (e.g. Buy, Get, Do, Call, Join, Drink, Taste, Come to, etc.)

- **Is there a specific response sought?** (Most ads: *to buy something.*)

- **If not:** is it *conditioning* ("public relations" or "image building") to make us **"feel good"** about the company, to get favorable public opinion on *its* side (against any government regulations, taxes)?

In the following pages, the three simple teaching devices *(the 30-Second-Spot Quiz; the Intensify/Downplay schema; Questions You Can Ask)* are all designed so that they may be photocopied by teachers and used in the classroom. They were originally created as part of my work with the National Council of Teachers of English (NCTE) Committee on Public Doublespeak. My intent was to create simple teaching devices to teach kids how to recognize patterns of persuasion, how to analyze propaganda. These pages are crammed with information, relatively self-contained and self-explanatory, and are designed to be easily photocopied by individuals and to be incorporated by other writers into their texts.

How to Analyze Ads:
Use this 1-2-3-4-5 sequence of questions, (see next page) to focus on the *"skeleton"* underneath the *"surface variations"* of radio and TV commercials, newspaper and magazine ads. ▶

Recognize that a 30-second TV ad is a **synthesis,** the end product of a complex process in which scores of people (writers, researchers, psychologists, artists, actors, camera crews, etc.) may have spent months putting together the details. TV commercials are often the best *compositions* of our age, skillful combinations of purposeful words and images. Be patient and systematic: **analysis** takes time to sort out all of the things going on at once. **We perceive** these things *simultaneously,* but we must discuss them *sequentially.* Use this 1-2-3-4-5 pattern of "the pitch" as a sequence to start your analysis.

THE 30-SECOND-SPOT QUIZ

Recognize "surface variations": in 30 seconds, a TV spot may have 40 quick-cut scenes of "good times" (happy people, sports fun, drinking cola); or one slow "tracking" scene of an old-fashioned sleighride through the woods, ending at "home" with "Season's Greetings" from an aerospace corporation; or a three-scene drama: a problem suffered by some "friend," a product/solution recommended by a trusted "authority," and a final grateful smile from the relieved sufferer. But, the structure underneath is basically the same.

Recognize our own involvement in a mutual transaction. Persuaders are *benefit-promisers,* but we are *benefit-seekers.* Most ads relate to simple "trade-offs" of mutual benefits: consumers get a pleasure, producers get a profit. However, investigate issues relating to any non-consumer ad; these are paid presentations of only one side of an issue, often involving more than a simple purchase transaction.

Understand that advertising is basically persuasion, not information nor education. *And not coercion!* Many important moral and ethical issues (concerning intent and consequences, priorities, individual and social effects, truth and deception, legal and regulatory problems) are related. The more we know about the basic techniques of persuasion, the better able we are not only to cope with the multiple persuaders in our society, but also to consider these ethical issues.

Based on **The Pitch** © 1982 by Hugh Rank

148   The Pitch

1 What ATTENTION-GETTING techniques are used?

Anything unusual? Unexpected? Noticeable? Interesting? Related to:
- ☐ **senses:** motions, colors, lights, sounds, music, visuals (e.g., computer graphics, slow-motion)
- ☐ **emotions:** any associations (*see list below*): sex, scenery, exciting action, fun, family, pets.
- ☐ **thought:** news, list, displays, claims, advice, questions, stories, demonstrations.

(*Popular TV* **programs** *function as* attention-getters to *"deliver the audience" to advertisers.)*

2 What CONFIDENCE-BUILDING techniques are used?

- ☐ Do you *recognize, know* (from earlier repetition) the **brand name? company? symbol? package?**
- ☐ Do you *already know, like* and *trust* the **"presenters"**: the endorsers, actors, models?
- ☐ Are these "presenters" **AUTHORITY FIGURES** (expert, wise, caring, protective?) Or, are they **FRIEND FIGURES** (someone you like, like to be, "on your side"; including "cute" cartoons)?
- ☐ What key **words** are used? *(Trust, sincere,* etc.) **Nonverbals?** *(smiles, voice tones, sincere look)*
- ☐ In **mail** ads, are computer-written *"personalized"* touches used? On **telephone:** tapes? scripts?

3 What DESIRE-STIMULATING techniques are used?   (main part of ad)

Consider (a) **"target audience"** as (b) **benefit-seeking;** and persuaders' benefit-promising strategies as focused on (c) **product claims,** or, (d) **"added values"** associated with product:

- ☐ a. **Who is the "target audience"?** Are *you?* (If *not,* as part of an unintended audience, are you *uninterested* or *hostile* toward the ad?)

- ☐ b. **What's the primary motive of that audience's benefit-seeking?** Use chart at right. Most ads are simple acquisition (*lower left*). Often, such motives co-exist, but one may be dominant. Ads which intensify a **problem,** (that is, a "bad" already hated or feared; *the opposite, or the absence of,* "goods") and then offer the product as a **solution,** are here called **"scare-and-sell"** ads. *(right side).*

To keep a "good" (protection)	To get rid of a "bad" (relief)
To get a "good" (acquisition)	To avoid a "bad" (prevention)

The 30-Second-Spot Quiz

☐ c. **What kinds of product claims are emphasized?** *(Use these 12 categories.)* What key words, images? Any *measurable* claims? Or are they *subjective opinions, generalized* praise words ("puffery")?

SUPERIORITY *("best")*
QUANITITY *("most")*
EFFICIENCY *("works")*
BEAUTY *("lovely")*
SCARCITY *("rare")*
NOVELTY *("new")*

STABILITY *("classic")*
RELIABILITY *("solid")*
SIMPLICITY *("easy")*
UTILITY *("practical")*
RAPIDITY *("fast")*
SAFETY *("safe")*

☐ d. **Are any "added values" implied or suggested?** Are there words or images which associate the product with some "good" already loved or desired by the intended audience? With such common human needs/wants/desires as in these 24 categories:

"basic needs:"
FOOD *("tasty")*
ACTIVITY *("exciting")*
SURROUNDINGS *("comfort")*
SEX *("alluring")*
HEALTH *("healthy")*
SECURITY *("protect")*
ECONOMY *("save")*

"certitude" needs:
RELIGION *("right")*
SCIENCE *("research")*
BEST PEOPLE *("elite")*
MOST PEOPLE *("popular")*
AVERAGE PEOPLE *("typical")*

"territory" needs:
NEIGHBORHOOD *("hometown")*
NATION *("country")*
NATURE *("earth")*

love & belonging needs:
INTIMACY *("lover")*
FAMILY *("Mom" "kids")*
GROUPS *("team")*

"growth" needs:
ESTEEM *("respected")*
PLAY *("fun")*
GENEROSITY *("gift")*
CREATIVITY *("creative")*
CURIOUSITY *("discover")*
COMPLETION *("success")*

4 Are there URGENCY-STRESSING techniques used?
(Not all ads: but always check.)

☐ If an urgency appeal: What words? *(e.g. Hurry, Rush, Deadline, Sale Ends, Offer Expires, Now.)*

☐ If **no** urgency: is this **"soft sell"** part of a *repetitive, long-term ad campaign* for standard item?

5 What RESPONSE-SEEKING techniques are used?

☐ Are there specific *triggering* words used? (Buy, Get, Do, Call, Act, Join, Smoke, Drink, Taste, etc.)

☐ Is there a **specific response** sought? (Most ads: to buy something)

☐ If **not:** is it **conditioning** ("public relations" or "image building") to make us **"feel good"** about the company, to get favorable public opinion on *its* side (against any government regulations, taxes)?

(Persuaders always seek some kind of response!)

Observe. Understand Judge. (In *that* sequence!) Observe closely what is explicitly said and shown; consider carefully what may be implied, suggested either by verbal or nonverbal means.

Anticipate incoming information. Have some way to sort, some place to store. If you know common patterns, you can pick up cues from bits and fragments, recognize the situation, know the probable options, infer the rest, and even note the omissions. Some persuaders use these techniques (and some observers analyze them) consciously and systematically; others, intuitively and haphazardly.

Categorize, but don't "pigeonhole." Things may be in many categories at the same time. "Clusters" and "mixes" are common. Observers often disagree.

Seek "dominant impressions," but relate them to the whole. You can't analyze *everything*. Focus on what seems *(to you)* the most *noticeable, interesting,* or *significant* elements (e.g. an intense "urgency" appeal, a very strong "authority" figure). By relating these to the whole context of "the pitch," your analysis can be *systematic, yet flexible,* appropriate to the situation.

Translate "indirect" messages. Much communication is *indirect,* through metaphoric language, allusions, rhetorical questions, irony, nonverbals (gestures, facial expressions, tone of voice), etc. Millions of specific concrete ways of communicating something can be grouped in the general abstract categories listed here as "product claims" (3c) and "common needs" (3d). Visuals imply.

Train yourself by first analyzing those ads which explicitly use the full sequence of "the pitch," including "urgency-stressing" and a specific "response-seeking." Always check for this full sequence; when it does not appear, consider what may have been omitted: *assumed* or *implied*. "Soft sell" ads and corporate "image-building" ads are harder to analyze: *less is said, more is implied.*

Practice. Analysis is a skill which can be learned, but it needs to be practiced. Take notes. Use print ads. Videotape, if possible; replay in slow motion. No one can "see" or "understand" everything during the actual 30 seconds while watching a TV spot. At best, we pick up a few impressions. Use the pattern of "the pitch" to organize your analysis and aid your memory. Such organization helps to avoid randomness and simple subjectivity.

Are ads worth all of this attention? Ads may not be, but *your mind is.* If we can better learn how to analyze things, to recognize patterns, to sort out incoming information, to see the parts, the processes, the structure, the relationships within things so common in our everyday environment, then it's worth the effort.

Readers will recognize that the **30-Second-Spot Quiz** is a summary or an epitome of this book. As such, it can be used as a quick reference by those who wish to analyze ads. In addition to the 1-2-3-4-5 sequence here, this quiz is sandwiched by two pages of tersely-written suggestions and guides on how to analyze ads.

The Intensify/Downplay schema was released in 1976 and has been used in many classrooms since then. Although it is the *most comprehensive* way to analyze ads, the 30-Second-Spot Quiz will probably be the *easiest* way for many people to start. In the "Composition" section of the schema, it notes the importance of *"the strategy of longer messages."* Here, I'll label the most common strategy of advertising as this 1-2-3-4-5 sequence of the "pitch," and have created a simply little quiz to focus on it. This quiz, and this method of analysis, can be applied to other media — print ads in magazines, newspapers, billboards, and so on — in addition to TV spots.

THE INTENSIFY/ DOWNPLAY SCHEMA

The **Intensify/Downplay schema** was originally published in *Teaching About Doublespeak* (Urbana: NCTE, 1976), designed as a simple device to teach propaganda analysis. Four years earlier, I had surveyed high school and college textbooks, finding out that *almost nothing* was being taught about propaganda, political and commercial persuasion. If anything, texts had a simple listing of "the 7 most common propaganda techniques" (glittering generalities, name-calling, etc.), a very inadequate list, or a listing of fallacies of formal logic.

After sorting and re-sorting some twenty five different lists and systems, reading a lot of advertising books, and watching a lot of TV, I produced this Intensify/Downplay schema which subsumes many of these lists. The intent was to create something *simple, useful, practical, accurate — and easily copied,* so that anyone with access to a Xerox machine could reproduce it whole. Since then, I've found that it remains a solid structure from which other patterns can be based: here, for example, the 30-Second-Spot Quiz, the Questions list, and the Reference Guide.

INTENSIFY

Repetition

Intensifying by repetition is an easy, simple, and effective way to persuade. People are comfortable with the *known,* the *familiar.* As children, we love to hear the same stories repeated; later, we have "favorite" songs, TV programs, etc. All cultures have chants, prayers, rituals, dances based on repetition. Advertising slogans, brand names, logos, and signs are common. Much education, training, indoctrination is based on repetition to imprint on the *memory* of the receiver to identify, recognize, and *respond.*

Association

Intensifying by linking (1) the idea or product with (2) something *already loved/desired by* - or *hated/feared by* (3) the intended audience. Thus, the need for **audience analysis:** surveys, polls, "market research," "consumer behavior," psychological and sociological studies. Associate by *direct* assertions or *indirect* ways; (metaphoric language, allusions, backgrounds, contexts, etc.) Some "good things" often linked with products are those common human needs/wants/desires for "basics," "certitude," "intimacy," "space," and "growth."

Composition

Intensifying by pattern and arrangement uses *design, variations in sequence* and *in proportion* to add to the force of words, images, movements, etc. How we put together, or compose, is important: e.g. in **verbal** communication: the choice of words, their level of abstraction, their patterns within sentences, the strategy of longer messages. Logic, inductive and deductive, puts ideas together systematically. **Non-verbal** compositions involve *visuals* (color, shape, size); *aural* (music); *mathematics* (quantities, relationships), *time* and *space* patterns.

The INTENSIFY/DOWNPLAY schema is a pattern useful to analyze communication, persuasion and propaganda. All people *intensify* (commonly by *repetition, association, composition*) and *downplay* (commonly by *omission, diversion, confusion*) as they communicate in words, gestures, numbers, etc. But, "professional persuaders" have more training, technology, money and media access than the average citizen. Individuals can better cope with organized persuasion by recognizing the common ways *how* communication is intensified or downplayed, and by considering *who is saying what to whom, when and where, with what intent and what result.*

DOWNPLAY

Omission

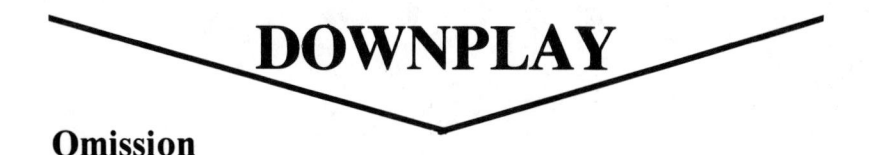

Downplaying by omission is common since the basic selection/omission process *necessarily omits* more than can be presented. All communication is limited, is edited, is slanted or biased to include and exclude items. But omission can also be used as a *deliberate* way of concealing, hiding. Half-truths, quotes out of context, etc. are very hard to detect or find. Political examples include *cover-ups, censorship, book-burning, managed news, secret police activities.* Receivers, too, can omit: can "filter out" or be closed minded, prejudiced.

Diversion

Downplaying by distracting focus, diverting attention away from key issues or important things; usually by intensifying the side-issues, the non-related, the trivial. Common variations include: "hair-splitting," "nit-picking," "attacking a straw man," "red herring"; also, those emotional attacks and appeals *(ad hominem, ad populum)*, plus things which drain the energy of others: *"busy work," "legal harassment,* etc. Humor and entertainment *("bread and circuses")* are used as pleasant ways to divert attention from major issues.

Confusion

Downplaying issues by making things so complex, so chaotic, that people "give up," get weary, "overloaded." This is dangerous when people are unable to understand, comprehend, or make reasonable decisions. Chaos can be the accidental result of a disorganized mind, or the deliberate flim-flam of a *con man* or the political *demagogue* (who then offers a "simple solution" to the confused). Confusion can result from *faulty logic, equivocation, circumlocution. contradictions, multiple diversions, inconsistencies, jargon* or anything which blurs clarity or understanding.

© **1976 by Hugh Rank. Permission to reprint for educational purposes hereby granted,** *pro bono publico. Endorsed by the Committee on Public Doublespeak, National Council of Teachers of English (NCTE).*

QUESTIONS YOU CAN ASK ABOUT ANY AD

In the following two-page spread is a list of some 200 questions which can be asked about any ad. Based on the Intensify/Downplay schema, this is another simple teaching device (designed to be photocopied) which may be useful in the classroom or at home.

Such a list is abstract and general; for more concrete and specific applications, use the **Reference Guide** section which shows how these questions can be applied to many different kinds of products and services.

The most interesting aspect of this list may be the systematic way it examines **omissions** by applying a traditional analysis of cause-and-effect, focusing on the various causes (material, efficient, formal, final) of harmful effects. Omissions are very hard to detect. It's very difficult to determine what *isn't* said. But this pattern is a useful starting point.

ads **INTENSIFY** the "good"
by means of repetition, association, composition

Repetition

How often have you seen the ad? On TV? In print? Do you recognize the **brand name? trademark? logo? company? package?** What key words or images repeated within ad? Any repetition patterns *(alliteration, anaphora, rhyme)* used? Any **slogan?** Can you hum or sing the **musical theme** or **jingle?** How long has this ad been running? How old were you when you first heard it? (For information on frequency, duration, and costs of ad campaigns, see *Advertising Age.)*

Association

What **"good things"** - already loved or desired by the intended audience - are associated with the product? Any links with basic needs *(food, activity, sex, security)?* With an appeal to save or gain money? With desire for certitude or outside approval (from *religion, science,* or the *"best," "most,"* or *"average" people)?* With desire for a sense of space *(neighborhood, nation, nature)?* With desire for love and belonging *(intimacy, family, groups)?* With other human desires *(esteem, play, generosity, curiosity, creativity, completion)?* Are **"bad things"** - things already hated or feared - stressed, as in a **"scare-and-sell"** ad? Are *problems* presented, with products as *solutions?* Are the speakers (models, endorsers) **authority figures:** people you respect, admire? Or **friend figures:** people you'd like as friends, identify with, or would like to be?

Composition

Look for the basic strategy of *"the pitch": Hi... TRUST ME... YOU NEED... HURRY... BUY.* What are the **attention-getting (HI)** words, images, devices? What are the **confidence-building (TRUST ME)** techniques: words, images, smiles, endorsers, brand names? Is the main **desire-stimulation (YOU NEED)** appeal focused on our benefit-seeking *to get* or *to keep* a *"good,"* or *to avoid* or *to get rid of* a *"bad"*? Are you the **"target audience"**? If not, who is? Are you part of an unintended audience? When and where did the ads appear? Are **product claims** made for: *superiority, quantity, beauty, efficiency, scarcity, novelty, stability, reliability, simplicity, utility, rapidity,* or *safety?* Are any **"added values"** suggested or implied by using any of the association techniques (see above)? Is there any **urgency-stressing (HURRY)** by words, movement, pace? Or is a "soft sell" conditioning for *later* purchase? Are there specific **response-triggering** words **(BUY):** to buy, to do, to call? Or is it conditioning (image building or public relations) to make us *"feel good"* about the company, to get favorable public opinion on *its* side *(against government regulations, laws, taxes)?* **Persuaders seek some kind of response!**

© 1982 by Hugh Rank. Permission granted to photocopy for classroom use.

Omission

What "bad" aspects, disadvantages, drawbacks, hazards, have been **omitted** from the ad? Are there some unspoken assumptions? An un-said story? Are some things implied or suggested, but not explicitly stated? Are there concealed problems concerning the **maker,** the **materials,** the **design,** the **use,** or the **purpose of the product? Are there any unwanted or harmful side effects:** *unsafe, unhealthy, uneconomical, inefficient, unneeded?* Does any **"disclosure law"** exist (or is needed) requiring public warning about a concealed hazard? In the ad, what gets less time, less attention, smaller print? *(Most ads are true, but incomplete.)*

Diversion

What benefits (low cost, high speed, etc.) get high priority in the ad's claim and promises? Are these **your** priorities? Significant, important to you? Is there any **"balt-and-switch"?** *(Ad stresses low cost, but the actual seller switches buyer's priority to high quality.)* Does ad divert focus from **key issues,** important things *(e.g. nutrition, health, safety)?* Does ad focus on **side-issues,** unmeaningful trivia *(common in parity products)?* Does ad divert attention from your other choices, other options: buy something else, use less, use less often, rent, borrow, share, do without? *(Ads need not show other choices, but* you *should know them.)*

Confusion

Are the words clear or ambiguous? Specific or vague? Are claims and promises absolute, or are there qualifying words *("may help," "some")?* Is the claim measurable? Or is it **"puffery"?** *(Laws permit most* "seller's talk" *of such general praise and subjective opinions.)* Are the words common, understandable, familiar? Uncommon? Jargon? Any parts difficult to "translate" or explain to others? Are analogies clear? Are comparisons within the same kind? Are examples related? Typical? Adequate? Enough examples? Any contradictions? Inconsistencies? Errors? Are there frequent changes, variations, revisions *(in size, price, options, extras, contents, packaging)?* Is it too complex: too much, too many? Disorganized? Incoherent? Unsorted? Any confusing statistics? Numbers? Do you know exact costs? Benefits? Risks? Are **your own goals,** priorities, and desires clear or vague? Fixed or shifting? Simple or complex? *(Confusion can also exist within us as well as within an ad. If any confusion exists: slow down, take care.)*

ads **DOWNPLAY** the "bad"
by means of omission, diversion, confusion

COMMON PRODUCTS & SERVICES

"Eat, drink and be wary"
- Soft Drinks
- Beer
- Liquor
- Cigarettes
- Candy
- Cereals
- Snack Foods
- Easy-Foods
- Fast Foods
- O-T-C Drugs

"Body Language"
"Body Work"
- Cosmetics
- Clothes

"Trinkets and Treasures"
- Cars
- Car Care
- Motorcycles
- Cameras
- Stereo
- LP Records
- Entertainments
- Hotels/Motels
- Airlines

"Coming of Age"
- Military Ads
- College Ads
- Job Ads
- Wedding Ads
- Self-Improvement
- Get-Rich-Quick

"Living Happily Ever After"
- Real Estate
- Home Repairs
- Furniture & Appliances
- Utilities
- Insurance
- Baby Care
- Toys
- Cleaning Aids
- Banks
- Credit Cards
- Funerals

Reference Guide

Use this section
as a handy guide:
► analyzing ads
► watching commercials
►.before buying

REFERENCE GUIDE

These 39 categories represent thousands of items and billions of dollars of advertising. To some people, the comments here are obvious; to others, not so. Skim through these pages. See what you can learn - not only about what ads **intensify**, by means of *repetition, association,* and *composition,* but also about what ads **downplay** - by *omission, diversion,* and *confusion.*

Anticipate what can be expected. Be able to articulate, to specify, to name, to categorize the content and form.

Use common sense. Effective ads will have *many* persuasive techniques appearing at the same time. Don't try to "pigeonhole" into one category. Seek *dominant impressions.* Note *common clusters,* such as RAPIDITY/SIMPLICITY ("quick and easy") or ACTIVITY/NOVELTY ("exciting new"). Be flexible. Some corporations will pitch to a dozen different target audiences; some Chevrolet ads, for example, may stress BEAUTY, others UTILITY; some for a "plain folks" audience, others for an "elite." Ads *need not* show the "bad" about the product, but *you should* be aware of these omissions and diversions. Opinions will differ as to what are the "key issues" -whether top priority should go to health, safety, cost, style, or whatever. Some people may think that *"it's worth it"* to buy some illusions. This book stresses **informed choice:** we should know what the "trade-offs" are. Here, each page acts as a framework for a systematic way of analysis.

INTENSIFY the "good"

▶ Ads often **repeat** *brand names & slogans* including: Coca Cola's "Coke adds life," "It's the real thing," "The pause that refreshes"; Pepsi's "Pepsi Generation"; Royal Crown's "Me and my RC"; Seven-Up's "The Uncola," "Undo it — with 7 Up"; and Dr. Pepper's "Be a Pepper!"

▶ Ads often **associate** items with things already desired by, or held favorably by the intended audience. Human needs commonly associated here include: FOOD ("tasty"); ACTIVITY ("lively," "youth"); SEX ("romance"); APPROVAL ("most people," "average people"); TERRITORY ("nature," "country," "hometown"); PLAY ("fun"); GENEROSITY ("treat"). BELONGING ("friends," "family").

▶ Ads are **composed** using key words and images intensifying the "good" of such common intrinsic qualities: SUPERIORITY ("tastes good," "best selling"); QUANTITY ("more," "bigger").

DOWNPLAY the "bad"

▶ Ads often **omit** *disadvantages* such as high sugar content; no nutritional value; caffine content; *Health Factors:* tooth decay, obesity, and high blood sugar levels; high cost per use -for flavored water.

▶ Ads often **divert** attention away from *key issues* (health) or *other choices* such as: buying other brands, powdered drink mixes, fruit juices, vegetable juices, iced tea or coffee, beer, alcoholic beverages, and water; buying less, buying less often, not buying.

▶ **Confusion** sometimes occurs in the pricing differences in can and bottle sizes; *packaging techniques* (six vs. eight packs).

INTENSIFY the "good"

▶ Ads often **repeat** *brand names & slogans* including: Michelob's "Weekends are made for Michelob"; Budweiser's "The King of Beers," "When you've said Budweiser, you've said it all"; Schlitz's "Gusto," "When you're out of Schlitz, you're out of beer". Nonverbals: Hamm's bear, Schlitz's Malt Liquor Bull.

▶ Ads often **associate** items with things already desired by, or held favorably by the intended audience. Human needs commonly associated here include: FOOD ("delicious") ACTIVITY ("lively"); SEX ("masculine"); APPROVAL ("most people," "average people"; NEIGHBORHOOD ("hometown"); BELONGING ("friends"); PLAY ("enjoy"); GENEROSITY ("share"). Typical "good times": male companionship, camraderie.

▶ Ads are **composed** using key words and images intensifying the "good" of such common intrinsic qualities: SUPERIORITY ("tastes great") ("finest ingredients"); STABILITY ("time-tested," traditional"). Heavy promotion in taverns (signs, clocks, lamps, etc.); on TV sports.

DOWNPLAY the "bad"

▶ Ads often **omit** *disadvantages* such as alcoholism, public safety problems (drunk driving); obesity (beer belly); expense; health problems (heart, liver, blood), hangovers; basic sameness in taste; mass-produced uniformity - 10 brewers supply 90% beer in U.S.A. Low-calorie beers use euphemisms (less-*filling*) for less-*fattening*.

▶ Ads often **divert** attention away from *key issues* (health and safety) as *other choices* such as: other brands of beer, soft drinks, wine, hard liquor, water, buying less, buying less often, not buying.

▶ **Confusion** sometimes occurs in the pricing differences in can and bottle sizes; *packaging techniques* (six vs. eight packs).

INTENSIFY the "good"

DOWNPLAY the "bad"

▶ Ads often **repeat** *brand names & slogans* including: Seagrams Seven Crown, Smirnoff Vodka, Bacardi Rum, V.O., Jim Beam, Gordon's Gin, J & B Scotch, Gilbey's Gin.

▶ Ads often **omit** *disadvantages* such as alcoholsim, public safety problems (drunk driving); obesity; expense; health problems (heart, liver, blood), hangovers; marital and family problems of drinkers.

▶ Ads often **associate** items with things already desired by, or held favorably by the intended audience. Human needs commonly associated here include: FOOD ("delicious"); ACTIVITY ("refreshing," "soothing"); SEX ("romantic"); APPROVAL ("best people," "most people," "average people"); BELONGING ("friends"); PLAY ("enjoy"); ESTEEM ("admired"); GENEROSITY ("gift").

▶ Ads often **divert** attention away from *key issues* (health and safety), or *other choices* such as: buying other brands, beer, wine, soft drinks, water; buying less, buying less often; not buying.

▶ Ads are **composed** using key words and images intensifying the "good" of such common intrinsic qualities: SUPERIORITY ("best tasting," "finest ingredients"); SCARCITY ("rare"); STABILITY ("classic"). Prohibited from TV and radio; many local sales limitations.

▶ **Confusion** sometimes occurs in the proof ratings (alcohol content), blends, bottle sizes, packaging (similar names and labels), shelf display.

INTENSIFY the "good"

▶ Ads often **repeat** *brand names & slogans* including: Marlboro's "Come to Marlboro Country"; Virginia Slims' "You've come a long way baby"; Winston, Kool; Salem, Kent, Pall Mall, Lucky Strike, etc.

▶ Ads often **associate** items with things already desired by, or held favorably by the intended audience. Human needs commonly associated here include: FOOD ("taste," "aroma"); SEX ("masculine," "feminine"); HEALTH ("filtered"); APPROVAL ("scientific," "best people," "most people," "average people");PLAY ("enjoy," "refreshing"); ESTEEM ("admired"); BELONGING ("friends").

▶ Ads are **composed** using key words and images intensifying the "good" of such common intrinsic qualities: SUPERIORITY ("tastes good"); NOVELTY ("exciting new"); EFFICIENCY (filter "really works"). Target audience: *indirectly,* young teenagers as new market; *directly,* filter ads geared at adults unable to quit smoking.

DOWNPLAY the "bad"

▶ Ads often **omit** *disadvantages* such as HEALTH PROBLEMS: cancer, emphysema, heart trouble, respiratory troubles, pre-natal damage; nicotine addiction, stained teeth; HIGH COST: odor on clothes and body, offensive and discourteous to non-smokers. (Since 1964, warning labels required by law; since 1971, no radio and TV ads).

▶ Ads often **divert** attention away from *key issues*: (health) or *other choices* -buying other brands, pipe tobacco, cigars, chewing tobacco or gum, buying less, buying less often, not buying.

▶ **Confusion** sometimes occurs in tar and nicotine content statistics; similarity of competing brand names *(True, Fact, Real,* etc.)

INTENSIFY the "good"

DOWNPLAY the "bad"

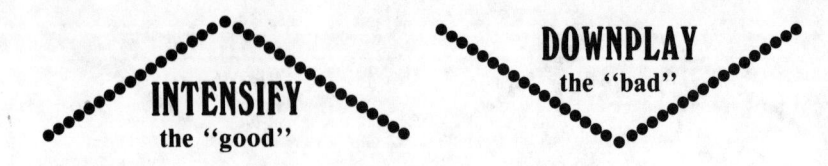

▶ Ads often **repeat** *brand names & slogans* including: M & M's melts in your mouth, not in your hands"; Wrigley Gum's "Double your pleasure, Double your fun with Doublemint, Doublemint, Doublemint Gum"; Snicker's' "like a fistful of peanuts in every bar"; and Mounds "Some times you feel like a nut, some times you don't."

▶ Ads often **associate** items with things already desired by, or held favorably by the intended audience. Human needs commonly associated here include: FOOD ("tasty," "sweet," "chewy"); ACTIVITY ("lively"); HEALTH ("wholesome"); APPROVAL ("most people," "average people"); NATURE ("natural"); BELONGING ("family," "friends"); PLAY ("fun"); GENEROSITY ("share," "treat").

▶ Ads are **composed** using key words and images intensifying the "good" of such common intrinsic qualities: SUPERIORITY ("goodness"); QUANTITY ("lots," "plenty"); NOVELTY ("exciting new"). Target audience: children. Boxed candies as adult gift item (Valentine's, Mother's Day).

▶ Ads often **omit** *disadvantages* such as questionable nutritional value, high cost, high sugar content, health risks: tooth decay, high blood sugar level, hypertension.

▶ Ads often **divert** attention away from *key issues* (nutrition), or *other choices* such as: buying other brands, salty snacks, nuts, seeds, granola, celery, carrots, sandwiches, cheese, buying less, buying less often, not buying.

▶ **Confusion** sometimes occurs in the *packaging* (sizes, portions).

CEREAL ADS

INTENSIFY the "good"

▶ Ads often **repeat** *brand names & slogans* including: Rice Crispies's "Snap, Crackle, Pop"; Frosted Flakes' "They're ggreat"! Wheaties, "Breakfast of Champions"; Sugar Smacks, Trix, Cap'n Crunch; Sugar Pops, Cheerios, etc.

▶ Ads often **associate** items with things already desired by, or held favorably by the intended audience. Human needs commonly associated here include: FOOD ("delicious," "crunchy"); ACTIVITY ("lively"); HEALTH ("wholesome"); NATURE ("natural"); BELONGING ("family," "friends"); PLAY ("fun"); ESTEEM ("winners"); GENEROSITY ("delight," "please").

▶ Ads are **composed** using key words and images intensifying the "good" of such common intrinsic qualities: SUPERIORITY ("tastes great"); QUANTITY ("more"); NOVELTY ("exciting new"); RAPIDITY ("fast," "instant"); SIMPLICITY ("easy," "convenient"). Target audience: children, mothers. Heavy in-store promotion: shelf space, coupons, premiums, cartoon packaging, etc.

DOWNPLAY the "bad"

▶ Ads often **omit** *disadvantages* such as lack of nutritional value; high sugar content; health problems: tooth decay, hypertension, high blood sugar levels; expensive food item; cereals usually *replace* rather than accompany other breakfast food.

▶ Ads often **divert** attention away from *key issues* (nutrition), or *other choices* such as: buying other brands, eggs, meat, hot cereals, pancakes, waffles, toast, french toast, fruit, cheese, yogurt, juices, buying less, buying less often, not buying.

▶ **Confusion** sometimes occurs in the pricing, *packaging* (box sizes), similarities between cereal grains.

INTENSIFY the "good"

DOWNPLAY the "bad"

▶ Ads often **repeat** *brand names & slogans* including: Pringles, Fritos, Doritos, Lay's Potato Chips, Bachman's Pretzels, Ritz Crackers, Cheese Nips, Wheat Thins, Twinkies, Ho-Hos, Ding-Dongs, Zingers; many national and local brands of cookies, crackers, chips, pop corn, etc.

▶ Ads often **associate** items with things already desired by, or held favorably by the intended audience. Human needs commonly associated here include: FOOD ("tasty," "crunchy," "crisp"); ACTIVITY ("lively"); HEALTH ("wholesome"); APPROVAL ("most people," "average people"); NATURE ("natural"); BELONGING ("family," "friends"); PLAY ("enjoy"); GENEROSITY ("share," "treats").

▶ Ads are **composed** using key words and images intensifying the "good" of such common intrinsic qualities: SUPERIORITY ("tastes great"); QUANTITY ("more," "bigger"); NOVELTY ("exciting new"); SIMPLICITY ("easy"). Target audience: children, mothers. Heavy in-store promotion (shelf space) and in schools, parks, etc.

▶ Ads often **omit** *disadvantages* such as poor nutritional value; high calories; obesity problems; high sugar content or high salt content; high cost; chemical additives; critics call much of this "junk food."

▶ Ads often **divert** attention away from *key issues* (nutrition), or *other choices* such as: purchasing other brands, fruits, candy nuts, seeds, other natural food snacks, sandwiches, "left overs," change habitual or compulsive behavior, buying less, buying less often, not buying.

▶ **Confusion** sometimes occurs in the pricing and packaging techniques (box sizes).

INTENSIFY
the "good"

DOWNPLAY
the "bad"

▶ Ads often **repeat** *brand names & slogans* including: (frozen dinners) Swanson, Stouffer's, Banquet, Weight Watchers, Sara Lee, Pepperidge Farm; Hamburger Helper, Cup-a-Soup; Cake and Cookie mixes, and other "convenience" foods.

▶ Ads often **associate** items with things already desired by, or held favorably by the intended audience. Human needs commonly associated here include: FOOD ("delicious"); ACTIVITY ("lively"); APPROVAL ("most people," "average people"); BELONGING ("home," "family"); GENEROSITY ("treats").

▶ Ads are **composed** using key words and images intensifying the "good" of such common intrinsic qualities: SUPERIORITY ("tastes great"); NOVELTY ("exciting new"); RAPIDITY ("fast," "instant"); SIMPLICITY ("easy," "convenient"); UTILITY ("sensible," "practical"). Target audience: single adults, couples, working mothers. Many ads in women's magazines.

▶ Ads often **omit** *disadvantages* such as high cost, poor nutritional quality, chemical additives and preservatives, bland taste, small portions.

▶ Ads often **divert** attention away from *key issues* (cost), or *other choices* such as: buying other brands, unprepared foods, fresh fruits and vegetables, home-cooked, home-baked meals, restaurant eating, buying less, buying less often, not buying.

▶ **Confusion** sometimes occurs in the pricing and packaging.

INTENSIFY the "good"

▶ Ads often **repeat** *brand names & slogans* including: McDonalds' "You deserve a break today"; Kentucky Fried Chicken's "It's finger lickin' good"; Burger King's "Have it your way"; Jack in the Box; Dairy Queen, Pizza Hut, Denny's, A & W, Bonanza, Ponderosa, Arby's, Wendy's Dunkin' Donuts, Red Lobster, IHOP, Sizzler, etc.

▶ Ads often **associate** items with things already desired by, or held favorably by the intended audience. Human needs commonly associated here include: FOOD ("delicious," "tasty"); ACTIVITY ("lively"); APPROVAL ("most people," "average people"); NEIGHBORHOOD ("local,"); BELONGING ("family," "friends"); PLAY ("enjoy," "fun"); GENEROSITY ("treat").

▶ Ads are **composed** using key words and images intensifying the "good" of such common intrinsic qualities: SUPERIORITY ("tastes great"; QUANTITY ("more," "bigger"); NOVELTY ("exciting," "new") RAPIDITY ("fast service"); SIMPLICITY ("easy," "convenient"); UTILITY ("practical," "sensible"). Target audience: family, working singles, travelers, youth, TV, radio commercials at mealtimes.

DOWNPLAY the "bad"

▶ Ads often **omit** *disadvantages* such as uniform mediocrity of meals; nutritional problems (often high-fat, high-salt, high-sugar, high-calorie, high-carbohydrates) especially in greasy fried foods; high cost; crowded "rush hour" periods; little variety.

▶ Ads often **divert** attention away from *key issues* (nutrition) or *other choices* such as: buying at other places, home cooked meals, grocery store items, snack food, dieting, buying less, buying less often, not buying.

▶ **Confusion** sometimes occurs in the pricing (main item cheap, "extras" expensive).

O-T-C DRUG ADS

INTENSIFY the "good"

▶ Ads often **repeat** *brand names* of non-prescription drugs (also called "patent medicines" or O-T-C, "over-the-counter" drugs): Bayer aspirin, St. Joseph aspirin, Excedrin, Bufferin, Anacin, Tylenol, Datril, Geritol, Sominex, NyQuil, etc.

▶ Ads often **associate** items with things already desired by, or held favorably by the intended audience. Human needs commonly associated here include: ACTIVITY ("lively," "soothe," "refreshing"); SURROUNDINGS ("warm," "comfortable"); HEALTH ("relief," "aids"); SECURITY ("prevent," "guard"); APPROVAL ("scientific research," "hospital studies"); NATURE ("natural"); BELONGING ("care," "protect," "family").

▶ Ads are **composed** using key words and images intensifying the "good" of such common intrinsic qualities: SUPERIORITY ("best"); QUANTITY ("more"); EFFICIENCY ("effective," "really works"); STABILITY ("traditional"); NOVELTY ("exciting new," "discovery"); RELIABILITY ("powerful," "prompt"); SIMPLICITY ("easy," "convenient"); UTILITY ("practical"); SAFETY ("tested"). Ads often intensify the "bad" aspects of pain, discomfort: "scare-and-sell." Target audience: people in pain.

DOWNPLAY the "bad"

▶ Ads often **omit** *disadvantages* such as dangers of abuse; chances of side-effects; higher costs than generic drugs.

▶ Ads often **divert** attention away from *key issues* (promotes a drug-reliant culture), or *other choices* such as: buying other brands, generic drugs, prescription drugs, natural remedies, buying less, buying less often, not buying.

▶ **Confusion** sometimes occurs in the vague, ambiguous advertising claims; technical labeling language, packaging and display techniques.

INTENSIFY the "good"

DOWNPLAY the "bad"

▶ Ads often **repeat** slogans about health and beauty; some "brand names" (Weight-Watchers) of nationally-franchised sellers, many local and small mail-order firms dealing in: weight reduction, muscle-building, breast development, health clubs, diet plans, charm schools, "fat farms," etc.

▶ Ads often **associate** items with things already desired by, or held favorably by the intended audience. Human needs commonly associated here include: ACTIVITY ("vivacious," "youthful"); SEX ("alluring," "sexy"); HEALTH ("wholesome," "in shape," "fitness"); APPROVAL ("medical experts," "best people"); BELONGING ("love," "attractive" "friends"); PLAY ("enjoy"); ESTEEM ("admired," "liked"); COMPLETION ("fulfill," "develop potential"). Ads often intensify the "bad": scare-and-sell techniques emphasizing "ugly fat," loneliness, etc.

▶ Ads are **composed** using key words and images intensifying the "good" of such common intrinsic qualities: SUPERIORITY ("best"); BEAUTY ("good looking"); EFFICIENCY ("really works"); NOVELTY ("amazing new"); STABILITY ("practical"); RAPIDITY ("fast"); SIMPLICITY ("easy"). Target audience: young adults, especially fat people.

▶ Ads often **omit** *disadvantages* such as overall cost - including services, extra products, travel, time, discomfort, the "pain" of dieting; the endurance, discipline, regularity, willpower; motivation necessary; possible side-effects of drugs, aids.

▶ Ads often **divert** attention away from *key issues* (calorie intake), or *other choices* such as: doctor's advice; other clubs or programs; school or YMCA/YWCA gym; advice in library books; individual dieting and exercise. "Bait-and-switch" diversion away from cheap "introductory offer" to expensive long-term program.

▶ **Confusion** sometimes occurs in such services and products in which "failure" can be blamed on individual not following *all* directions, etc. Confusing language in ads, vague claims and promises, confusing number of programs, costs.

INTENSIFY the "good"

DOWNPLAY the "bad"

▶ Ads often **repeat** *brand* names of perfume, lipstick, powder, skin creme, eye makeup, deodorant, shampoo, hair spray, hair coloring, etc. including: Revlon, Avon, Max Factor, Cover Girl, Estee Lauder, Jovan, Ban, Secret, Right Guard, Dial, Breck, Adorn, Long and Silky, Short'n Sassy, etc.

▶ Ads often **associate** items with things already desired by, or held favorably by the intended audience. Human needs commonly associated here include: ACTIVITY ("youthful," "vivacious"); SEX ("alluring"); HEALTH ("wholesome"); SECURITY ("protect," "take care of"); APPROVAL ("best people," "most people," "average people"); NATURE ("natural"); BELONGING ("intimate"); PLAY ("enjoy"); ESTEEM ("admired"); GENEROSITY ("gift").

▶ Ads are **composed** using key words and images intensifying the "good" of such common intrinsic qualities: SUPERIORITY ("best"); BEAUTY "adorable"); EFFICIENCY ("really works"); NOVELTY ("exciting new"); STABILITY ("classic"); SCARCITY ("exclusive"). Target audience: women primarily, but now doubling market by selling male cosmetics - with "virile," outdoorsy, sporty names.

▶ Ads often **omit** *disadvantages* such as high cost; basic sameness in ingredients; application skill needed; chemical ingredients, danger of allergic reactions; real youth and beauty (of the models) cannot be bought.

▶ Ads often **divert** attention away from *key issues*, or *other choices* such as: buying other brands, home-made make-up, buying less, buying less often; not buying.

▶ **Confusion** sometimes occurs in the vague claims regarding results; label language; packaging; multiplicity of similar products, names, packages, claims.

INTENSIFY
the "good"

▶ Ads often **repeat** *brand names & slogans* of *products* (Arrow shirts, Adidas shoes, Levi's) or *stores* (Saks, Marshall Field's, the Gap, Simply Britches, etc.).

▶ Ads often **associate** items with things already desired by, or held favorably by the intended audience. Human needs commonly associated here include: ACTIVITY ("youthful"); SURROUNDINGS ("warmth") SEX ("attractive") APPROVAL ("best people" - for fashions, "most people" and "average people" for fads and casual clothes); BELONGING ("friends"); ESTEEM ("admired").

▶ Ads are **composed** using key words and images intensifying the "good" of such common intrinsic qualities: SUPERIORITY ("best"); BEAUTY ("good looking"); NOVELTY ("contemporary," "fashionable"); STABILITY ("classic"); RELIABILITY ("durable"); SCARCITY ("exclusive"); SIMPLICITY ("easy-care"); UTILITY ("practical").

DOWNPLAY
the "bad"

▶ Ads often **omit** *disadvantages* such as high costs; basic sameness in stores: high cleaning costs; products or size availability; quality of materials and sewing; cost of accessories needed; "cost-per-use" downplayed.

▶ Ads often **divert** attention away from *key issues* (utility, style) or *other choices* such as: buying other brands or at other stores; substitutes: used clothing, making your own; buying less new clothes; buying less often; not buying.

▶ **Confusion** sometimes occurs in the highly-inflated prices of fad and new fashion items: no base for judging a genuine sale or bargain; some confusion in fabrics, labels, sizes, care.

CAR ADS

▲ INTENSIFY the "good"

- ▶ Ads often **repeat** *brand names & slogans* including: Ford ("Ford has a better idea"); Chevrolet ("See the USA in your Chevrolet"); Datsun ("Datsun saves"); Buick; Cadillac; Lincoln; Mercury; Chrysler; Plymouth; Dodge; Oldsmobile; Pontiac; AMC; Volkswagen; Toyota; Fiat, etc.
- ▶ Ads often **associate** items with things already desired by, or held favorably by the intended audience. Human needs commonly associated here include: ACTIVITY ("lively"); SEX ("attractive"); APPROVAL ("scientific," "best people," "most people," "average people"); BELONGING ("lover," "family," "friends"); PLAY ("fun"); ESTEEM ("respect"); much attention given to car *names* for their favorable associations (fast animals, prestige locations, etc.).
- ▶ Ads are **composed** using key words and images intensifying the "good" of such common intrinsic qualities: SUPERIORITY ("best"); QUANTITY ("more"); BEAUTY ("handsome"); EFFICIENCY ("really works"); NOVELTY ("all new"); STABILITY ("classic"); RELIABILITY ("well-built"); RAPIDITY ("fast"); SIMPLICITY ("carefree"); UTILITY ("useful"); SAFETY ("protection"). Diverse ad strategy for nearly all "needs" and types.

▼ DOWNPLAY the "bad"

- ▶ Ads often **omit** *disadvantages* such as high cost; high cost of financing, extras, upkeep, repairs, gas, insurance; fast depreciation of value, safety factors (especially small cars), known defects and problems often concealed until an enforced "recall." Used cars: often conceal former use, existing defects, relative high cost and financing.
- ▶ Ads often **divert** attention away from *key issues* (safety), or *other choices* such as: buying other brands (of cars); using substitutes (bus, train, taxi, motorcycle, moped, bicycle, car pools, walking); buying used car, buying new car less often, not buying. *"Bait-and-switch" diversion very common:* low-priced cars advertised, then sellers persuade buyers to high-priced cars.
- ▶ **Confusion** sometimes occurs in the wide choice of options, extras, models, sizes, services, etc. Confusing numbers, prices; confusing technical jargon; confusing trade-in deals. Often very skilled persuaders selling: unequal situation.

INTENSIFY the "good"

▶ Ads often **repeat** *brand names & slogans* of gasoline (Shell, Standard, Amoco), tires (Goodyear, Goodrich, Firestone), batteries, mufflers, auto parts, accessories, waxes, services ("Mr. Goodwrench"), etc.

▶ Ads often **associate** items with things already desired by, or held favorably by the intended audience. Human needs commonly associated here include: SECURITY ("protect"); APPROVAL ("scientific," "technicians," "most people," "average people"). Some scare-and-sell intensifying "bad" of tire blow-outs, accidents.

▶ Ads are **composed** using key words and images intensifying the "good" of such common intrinsic qualities: SUPERIORITY ("best"); QUANTITY ("more"); EFFICIENCY ("really works"); NOVELTY ("all new"); STABILITY ("experienced"); RELIABILITY ("sturdy," "long- lasting"); RAPIDITY ("quick service"); SIMPLICITY ("automatic"); UTILITY ("practical"); SAFETY ("tested").

DOWNPLAY the "bad"

▶ Ads often **omit** *disadvantages* such as high cost; time delays; parts often unavailable; mechanics often not skilled or trained; basic sameness of gasoline.

▶ Ads often **divert** attention away from *key issues* (parity products do not vary; service and skill vary widely) or *other choices* such as: buying services or parts from competitors, buying a new car, self-repair; buying less non-essential items, or less often, or not buying.

▶ **Confusion** sometimes occurs in technical jargon used in ads and used by repairers; customer urgent need and lack of technical knowledge creates a very unequal situation; imitation ("gypsy") parts often sold; some "tourist-trap" frauds on highways; the *most common* consumer complaint is auto-repair.

INTENSIFY the "good"

▶ Ads often **repeat** *brand names & slogans* including: Kawasaki ("Let's the good times roll"), Suzuki, Yamaha, Honda, Harley-Davidson.

▶ Ads often **associate** items with things already desired by, or held favorably by the intended audience. Human needs commonly associated here include: ACTIVITY ("exciting," "thrilling," "adventure"); SEX ("masculine," "virile"); APPROVAL ("technical," "mechanics," "best people" -daring); NATURE ("outdoors"); BELONGING ("friends," "group"); PLAY ("fun"); ESTEEM ("noticed," "admired"); ECONOMY ("save gas, money").

▶ Ads are **composed** using key words and images intensifying the "good" of such common intrinsic qualities: SUPERIORITY ("best"); QUANTITY ("more"); BEAUTY ("handsome"); EFFICIENCY ("powerful"); NOVELTY ("exciting, new"); RELIABILITY ("rugged"); SCARCITY ("unique"); RAPIDITY ("fast"); UTILITY ("go-anywhere"). Target audience: young men.

DOWNPLAY the "bad"

▶ Ads often **omit** *disadvantages* such as danger, high safety risk, high accident rate for new owners; high insurance costs; limited use, or none in severe weather or winter; "cost-per-use" factor is often very high; cost of protective clothing; often restricted from "protected" outdoor areas.

▶ Ads often **divert** attention away from *key issues* (safety), or *other choices* such as: buying other brands, renting or borrowing, buying a car, not buying.

▶ **Confusion** sometimes occurs in the technical jargon; wide choice of models, options, sizes, similarities among brands.

INTENSIFY
the "good"

▶ Ads often **repeat** *brand names* including: Kodak, Polaroid, Nikon, Minolta, Olympus, Pentax, Yashica, Vivitar, Hasselblad.

▶ Ads often **associate** items with things already desired by, or held favorably by the intended audience. Human needs commonly associated here include: SEX ("alluring"); ECONOMY ("only"); APPROVAL ("experts" "favorite"); BELONGING ("love," "family," "friends"); PLAY ("enjoy"); ESTEEM ("admired"); GENEROSITY ("gift," "sharing"); CURIOUSITY ("discover," "fascinating"); COMPLETION ("fulfill"); CREATIVITY ("artistic," "craftsmanship").

▶ Ads are **composed** using key words and images intensifying the "good" of such common intrinsic qualities: SUPERIORITY ("best"); QUANTITY ("complete," "feature-packed"); EFFICIENCY ("really works," "results"); NOVELTY ("exciting new," "advanced"); STABILITY ("classic") RELIABILITY ("dependable," "authorized dealer," "well-built"); SCARCITY ("rare," "exclusive"); RAPIDITY ("instant'); SIMPLICITY ("automatic"); UTILITY ("practical").

DOWNPLAY
the "bad"

▶ Ads often **omit** *disadvantages* such as film and processing costs; high cost of repairs; cost of accessories; most "extras" seldom used; basic sameness among competing models.

▶ Ads often **divert** attention away from *key issues* (cost) or *other choices* such as: buying other brands; used cameras; renting, borrowing; hiring a photographer; buying cameras and film less often; buying less expensive models; not buying.

▶ **Confusion** sometimes occurs in selling expensive sophisticated equipment; technical jargon, acronymns, statistics; compairson-shipping is difficult because of price combinations, variations of features (lens, accessories, size); "list price" (like autos) is inflated in order to have cut-price sales.

INTENSIFY the "good"

DOWNPLAY the "bad"

▶ Ads often **repeat** brand names of speakers, receivers, turntables, systems: Advent, AIWA, Genesis, Hitachi, Infinity, Jensen, Pioneer, Sansui, Scott, Sherwood, SONY, etc. - or hi-fi store names, Musicraft, Playback, Pacific Stereo, etc. Many puns in slogans: *"sounds* good, "a *sound* investment."

▶ Ads often **associate** items with things already desired by, or held favorably by the intended audience. Human needs commonly associated here include: ACTIVITY ("youthful"); SEX ("attractive"); ECONOMY ("only"); APPROVAL ("scientific," "electronic," "best people," "most people"); BELONGING ("friends"); PLAY ("enjoy," "entertaining"); ESTEEM ("admired"); CREATIVITY ("artistic").

▶ Ads are **composed** using key words and images intensifying the "good" of such common intrinsic qualities: SUPERIORITY ("best"); QUANTITY ("more"); BEAUTY ("elegant"); EFFICIENCY ("really works"); NOVELTY ("advanced," "state-of-the-art"); STABILITY ("classic"); RELIABILITY ("dependable"); SCARCITY ("unique"); SIMPLICITY ("automatic"); UTILITY ("versatile"). Target audience: young adults.

▶ Ads often **omit** *disadvantages* such as high initial cost; high cost of tapes, records; repair or replacement costs; credit or financing cost; delivery and installation cost, antenna and wiring; FM reception poor in some areas; often people buy "more" sound than their home, room, or ears can receive without distortion.

▶ Ads often **divert** attention away from *key issues* (cost) or from *other choices* such as: buying other brands, buying used equipment, making own stereo (kit); buying less expensive model; not buying. "Bait and switch" very common diversion: ads for low-priced item bring buyers into store, then seller "switches" to other items.

▶ **Confusion** sometimes occurs in the use of technical jargon; marginal differences among various models, types, styles; judgment about quality of sound is very subjective; "list prices" are fictitiously inflated 30-40% in order to have cut-price "sales."

INTENSIFY
the "good"

DOWNPLAY
the "bad"

▶ Ads often **repeat** melodies, lyrics, performers names; most "advertising" is *indirect* by providing free records to AM and FM radio stations (and sometimes bribes — "payola," cash or drugs) to influence what songs are played. Recording industry is bigger, more profitable than movies.

▶ Ads often **associate** items with things already desired by, or held favorably by the intended audience. Human needs commonly associated here include: ACTIVITY ("exciting new"); SEX ("love"); ECONOMY ("only"); APPROVAL ("best people" - DJs, singers, bands; "most people," "average people"); BELONGING ("lover," "friends"); CREATIVITY ("artistic"). Many nonverbal associations (clothing, music styles); "insider" drug slang directed at youth sub-culture.

▶ Ads are **composed** using key words and images intensifying the "good" of such common intrinsic qualities: SUPERIORITY ("greatest"); QUANTITY ("more"); NOVELTY ("latest," "newest"); STABILITY ("classic"); SCARCITY ("collector's item"). Album cover artwork an important selling-point. Target audience: youth 10-17, 18-35.

▶ Ads often **omit** *disadvantages* such as high cost for "top" new records; often only one "hit" or one good side in a whole album; today's "favorites" are often boring tomorrow; cost-per-use.

▶ Ads often **divert** attention away from *key issues* (cost) or *other choices* such as: listening to the radio; tape-recording off the radio; borrowing or sharing records; buying less expensive, buying less often, not buying.

▶ **Confusion** sometimes occurs in pricing, labeling, packaging; similarity of names, "sounds," album covers; in mail-order record-club membership obligations, etc.

ENTERTAINMENT ADS

▲ INTENSIFY the "good"

▼ DOWNPLAY the "bad"

▶ Ads often **repeat** names of "stars," involved in movies, plays, concerts; sports (football, racing, etc.); fairs, amusement parks (Disney, etc.). Much indirect advertising as part of the "news". Often *selling* ephemeral *experience*, *memory* and *status* ("I saw . . . I was there") as an eye-witness.

▶ Ads often **associate** items with things already desired by, or held favorably by the intended audience. Human needs commonly associated here include: ACTIVITY ("exciting," "thrilling," "adventure"); SEX ("alluring"); ECONOMY ("only"); APPROVAL ("best people," "most people," "average people"); TERRITORY ("outdoors"); BELONGING ("friends"); PLAY ("enjoy"); ESTEEM ("admired"); GENEROSITY ("share"); CURIOSITY ("discover"); CREATIVITY ("artistic").

▶ Ads are **composed** using key words and images intensifying the "good" of such common intrinsic qualities: SUPERIORITY ("all-star"); QUANTITY ("more"); BEAUTY ("fabulous"); NOVELTY ("new," "premier"); STABILITY ("classic"); SCARCITY ("only appearance," "game of the year," "limited seating").

▶ Ads often **omit** *disadvantages* such as high total cost ("extras," parking, minimum and cover charge); unpleasant conditions (poor seats, crowds, long lines, bad weather, traffic, parking, etc.); brief appearances by "stars." No refunds if the experience is unsatisfactory.

▶ Ads often **divert** attention away from *key issues* (cost) or *other choices* such as: home recreation, radio, records, participating in games and athletics; watching the event on TV; attending fewer entertainments.

▶ **Confusion** sometimes occurs in a sudden blitz or hype of unknown, unreviewed movies; concerts, races, prizefights, or appearances of people with names similar to "stars," etc.

INTENSIFY the "good"

DOWNPLAY the "bad"

▶ Ads often **repeat** *brand names* and *slogans* including: Sheraton ("What has Sheraton done for you lately?"); Holiday Inn ("The World's Inn Keeper); Ramada Inn ("We're building our reputation, not resting on one"); Mariott, Hyatt, Pick, Americana, Stouffer, Travelodge, Days Inn, Rodeway Inns, Howard Johnson's, Best Western, etc.

▶ Ads ofen **associate** items with things already desired by, or held favorably by the intended audience. Human needs commonly associated here include: FOOD ("delicious"); ACTIVITY ("lively"); SURROUNDINGS ("comfortable"); APPROVAL ("best people," "most people," "average people"); BELONGING ("family," "friends"); PLAY ("enjoy"); ESTEEM ("honored," "status"); CURIOSITY ("discover," "explore").

▶ Ads are **composed** using key words and images intensifying the "good" of such common intrinsic qualities: SUPERIOR ("best"); QUANTITY ("more"); BEAUTY ("charming," "elegant"); NOVELTY ("modern"); RELIABILITY ("experienced," "dependable"); SCARCITY ("exclusive," "limited"); SIMPLICITY ("easy"); UTILITY ("practical"); SAFETY ("rest assured").

▶ Ads often **omit** disadvantages such as high costs; extra charges (tax, tips); reservations needed; inconvenient locations; small rooms; noise and traffic; views obstructed. National chains usually cost more than local hotels/motels in same area.

▶ Ads often **divert** attention away from *key issues* or *other choices* such as: staying at other hotels/motels; staying with friends or relatives; camping out, driving straight through.

▶ **Confusion** sometimes occurs in quoting cheapest rates "per-person, double occupancy"; in seasonal rate policies (off-season, on season); services included.

AIRLINE ADS

▲ INTENSIFY the "good"

▼ DOWNPLAY the "bad"

▶ Ads often **repeat** *brand names* and *slogans* including: American ("We're American Airlines doing what we do best"); Continental ("We really move our tail for you"); Delta ("Delta is ready when you are"); United ("Fly the friendly skies of United"); Eastern ("The Wings of Man"); TWA, Pan Am, Northwest Orient, etc.

▶ Ads often **associate** items with things already desired by, or held favorably by the intended audience. Human needs commonly associated here include: ACTIVITY ("adventure"); SURROUNDINGS ("comfort"); ECONOMY ("only"); APPROVAL ("scientific," "technical," "best people," "most people," "average people"); TERRITORY ("country," "national"); BELONGING ("family," "friends"); PLAY ("enjoy"); ESTEEM ("leader"); CURIOSITY ("discover," "explore").

▶ Ads are **composed** using key words and images intensifying the "good" of such common intrinsic qualities: SUPERIORITY ("best"); QUANTITY ('most,"); EFFICIENCY ("on time," "skilled"); NOVELTY ("modern"); STABILITY ("experienced," "proven"); RELIABILITY ("powerful,"); RAPIDITY ("fast"); SIMPLICITY ("convenient"); UTILITY ("practical"); SAFETY ("sure," "certain").

▶ Ads often **omit** disadvantages such as high cost; airport delays; baggage problems; overbooking; missed connections; rough weather, turbulent flights; safety risks, disasters; fear of flying.

▶ Ads often **divert** attention away from *key issues* (safety), or *other choices* such as: flying other airlines, traveling by train, bus, car; flying less often, not flying.

▶ **Confusion** often occurs in the complex rate/prices charged, discounts, package plans, tours, rebates, services offered, etc.

INTENSIFY the "good"

▶ Military service ads **repeat** common themes: benefit to individual in training, new skills, jobs, careers; adventure and travel; patriotism, service to country.

▶ Ads often **associate** items with things already desired by, or held favorably by the intended audience. Human needs commonly associated here include: ACTIVITY ("exciting," "adventure"); SEX ("manly"); SECURITY ("protector"); ECONOMY ("all-expenses"); APPROVAL ("best people," "most people," "average people"); NATION ("country," "serve"); BELONGING ("friends," "join"); PLAY ("fun"); ESTEEM ("respect," "admired,"); GENEROSITY ("help"); CURIOSITY ("explore," "discover"); COMPLETION ("achieve").

▶ Ads are **composed** using key words and images intensifying the "good" of such common intrinsic qualities: SUPERIORITY ("best"); QUANTITY ("more"); EFFICIENCY ("skilled"); NOVELTY ("advanced"); STABILITY ("heritage"); RELIABILITY ("rugged") SCARCITY ("special"); SIMPLICITY ("easy"). Target audience: young people via school assemblies, posters, displays, tours, direct mail, print ads, radio-TV, local recruiter.

DOWNPLAY the "bad"

▶ Ads often **omit** disadvantages such as danger in combat; restricted freedom, submission to authority, rules, orders; separation from family and friends; contract duration and penalties; living conditions; hard jobs, dull jobs; problems of veterans.

▶ Ads often **divert** attention away from *key issues*, or *other choices* such as: joining other branches of service; going to college or trade school, working, not enlisting.

▶ **Confusion** often occurs in the spoken promises of recruiters not binding; written contracts often specify skill *training*, (short term) but do not guarantee long-term placement, etc.

COLLEGE ADS

INTENSIFY the "good"

▶ College recruiting ads often **repeat** college name and common themes: *small colleges* -"personal attention," friendly, closeness to faculty and other students; *large universities* - opportunity, diversity, scope of program and activities; *all* are future-oriented (careers, success); *most* praise "well-rounded" student.

▶ Ads often **associate** items with things already desired by, or held favorably by the intended audience. Human needs commonly associated here include: ACTIVITY ("exciting"); SEX ("attractive"); ECONOMY ("investment,"); APPROVAL ("scientific," "best people,"); TERRITORY ("campus,"); BELONGING ("friends," "teams," "clubs"); PLAY ("fun"); ESTEEM ("success,"); CURIOSITY ("learn," "discover,"); COMPLETION ("achieve," "accomplish"); CREATIVITY ("artistic").

▶ Ads are **composed** using key words and images intensifying the "good" of such common intrinsic qualities: SUPERIORITY ("best"); QUANTITY ("more"); BEAUTY ("beautiful"); NOVELTY ("modern,"); STABILITY ("traditional,"); SCARCITY ("unique"); SIMPLICITY ("convenient"); UTILITY ("practical"). Target audience: high school students (after SAT tests) via posters, pamphlets, "fairs," phone calls, direct mailings, visits.

DOWNPLAY the "bad"

▶ Ads often **omit** disadvantages such as: (*small colleges*) inadequate facilities, science labs, library; understaffed programs, small faculty spread thin; (*large universities*) large class-size; freshman sections taught by grad students; (*All*): stress, homesickness; poor housing conditions, noise, traffic, parking; any *unfavorable* "outside" opinions or external evaluations.

▶ Ads often **divert** attention away from *key issues* (individual talent, motivation) or *other choices* such as: military service, working, part-time schooling at night, by mail, credit by examination; reading and self-teaching; no schooling.

▶ **Confusion** often occurs in the huge number of choices about colleges, programs, locations, features; in academic requirements, grading systems, scheduling; in administrative procedures, forms applications, financial aid, frequently changing and not standardized. Academic *jargon* can be used to inflate image, or to conceal anything. Some schools raise prices then offer many "discounts" calling them "scholarships" appealing to family pride.

INTENSIFY the "good"

▶ Job ads, from employment agencies or individual employers, often **repeat** common *themes*: opportunity, career, growth, future potential.

▶ Ads often **associate** items with things already desired by, or held favorably by the intended audience. Human needs commonly associated here include: ACTIVITY ("exciting"); SURROUNDINGS ("comfortable"); SEX ("attractive"); ECONOMY ("earn"); APPROVAL ("best people," "most people"); TERRITORY ("local," "hometown"); BELONGING ("friendly"); ESTEEM ("admired," "appreciated"); CURIOSITY ("interesting"); COMPLETION ("accomplish," "achieve"); CREATIVITY ("make").

▶ Ads are *composed* using key words and images intensifying the "good" of such common intrinsic qualities: SUPERIORITY ("best"); QUANTITY ("most"); BEAUTY ("glamorous"); EFFICIENCY ("competent"); NOVELTY ("modern"); STABILITY ("experienced"); RELIABILITY ("dependable"); SCARCITY ("unique"); RAPIDITY ("fast"); SIMPLICITY ("convenient"); UTILITY ("practical").

DOWNPLAY the "bad"

▶ Ads often **omit** disadvantages such as high cost for "placement fee" (often 10% of first year's salary); high cost for some "counseling services" to give simple common-sense advice; some jobs are paid by "sales commissions" (no salary); euphemisms ("Assistant Manager") used for low-paying jobs; omission of the job's disadvantages: risk, difficulty, distance, low pay, odd hours, etc.

▶ Ads often **divert** attention away from *other choices* such as: using a competing agency, the state employment agency, applying directly to employers; seeking guidance from public schools, free library sources.

▶ **Confusion** often occurs in the jargon and abbreviations in ads; in the skills or qualifications needed; in the duties performed. High risk fraud in some employment agencies and "training schools." Comparison shopping and search-time very important for any job seeker.

WEDDING ADS

▼ INTENSIFY the "good"

▼ DOWNPLAY the "bad"

▶ Ads often **repeat** brand names of products and local services related to weddings and new households: formalwear (Gingiss); diamonds ("A diamond is forever."); jewelers; caterers, printers, florists; photographers; travel; hotels; gifts; furniture; appliances; home.

▶ Ads often **associate** items with things already desired by, or held favorably by the intended audience. Human needs commonly associated here include: ACTIVITY ("exciting"); SEX ("romance"); ECONOMY ("affordable"); APPROVAL ("best people," "most people"); TERRITORY ("hometown," "local"); BELONGING ("family," "friends"); PLAY ("celebrate," "joy"); ESTEEM ("respected," "admired"); GENEROSITY ("gift," "cherished"); COMPLETION ("fulfill").

▶ Ads are *composed* using key words and images intensifying the "good" of such common intrinsic qualities: SUPERIORITY ("best"); QUANTITY ("most"); BEAUTY ("adorable," "charming"); EFFICIENCY ("capable"); NOVELTY ("exciting new"); STABILITY ("traditional"); RELIABILITY ("dependable"); SCARCITY ("rare"); SIMPLICITY ("easy"); UTILITY ("useful").

▶ Ads often **omit** disadvantages such as total wedding cost; high cost-per-use of some items; vulnerable time for impulse buying, buying spree, and the start of a debt cycle.

▶ Ads often **divert** attention away from *key issues* (the long-term relationship) or *other choices* such as: buying services from a competitor, buying substitutes (family party, home cooking, friend photographer, borrowed gown, etc.); informal wedding; elope.

▶ **Confusion** often occurs in the details of a package deal, vague description of services provided, hidden extras; "traditions" created by the sellers; highly emotional situation - unduly susceptible newlyweds unaccustomed to "comparison shopping" at very time when most major purchases are made.

INTENSIFY the "good"

▶ Ads often **repeat** common themes: *future* change, growth, improvement, "success" *after* buying, joining, *and* believing, following instructions. (If no success, buyer often feels that "belief" wasn't strong enough.) Products and services include books, courses, programs: *to improve "emotional life"* -meditation, positive thinking, assertiveness, biofeedback, encounter groups, TA, est, yoga; *to improve "social life"* -charm schools, modeling lessons, "success" and "popularity" clinics, etc.

▶ Ads often **associate** items with things already desired by, or held favorable by the intended audience. Human needs commonly associated here include: ACTIVITY ("alert," "vital"); APPROVAL ("best people"); BELONGING ("friends"); PLAY ("happiness"); ESTEEM ("admired"); CURIOSITY ("discover," "explore," "learn"); COMPLETION ("fulfill," "solve"); CREATIVITY ("create").

▶ Ads are **composed** using key words and images intensifying the "good" of such common intrinsic qualities: SUPERIORITY ("authentic," "genuine"); QUANTITY ("more"); BEAUTY ("beautiful"); EFFICIENCY ("really works"); NOVELTY ("exciting new," "advanced"); STABILITY ("traditional"); SCARCITY ("unique"); UTILITY ("practical").

DOWNPLAY the "bad"

▶ Ads often **omit** disadvantages such as high total cost (including extras, "advanced" programs, time involved); skill or discipline needed is often downplayed; results not sure, nor measurable: "feeling better" is very subjective.

▶ Ads often **divert** attention from *other choices* such as: improving one's self by other plans and programs; by more traditional programs offered by churches and philosophers; staying "unimproved."

▶ **Confusion** often occurs in the high-level abstract language used to describe goals and ideals; in the psychological jargon used; in the mixture of "true believers" and commercial exploitation involved in such self-improvement plans.

GET-RICH-QUICK ADS

INTENSIFY the "good"

▶ Ads often **repeat** common themes: *future* money or fame, *after* buying or investing, *and* working hard. (If the scheme fails, buyer often blames self for not working "hard enough.") Such "business opportunities" include commission sales, franchises, home jobs (stuffing envelopes, crafts, raising animals), "vanity press" for writers, "auditions" for singers, "patent advice" for inventors, etc.

▶ Ads often **associate** items with things already desired by, or held favorably by the intended audience. Human needs commonly associated here include: ACTIVITY ("exciting," "enthusiasm"); ECONOMY ("invest," "profitable"); APPROVAL ("best people"); BELONGING ("team," "join"); ESTEEM ("admired"); CURIOSITY ("discover," "secret of success," "inside information"); COMPLETION ("achieve"); CREATIVITY ("make").

▶ Ads are **composed** using key words and images intensifying the "good" of such common intrinsic qualities: SUPERIORITY ("best"); QUANTITY ("more"); EFFICIENCY ("really works," "results"); NOVELTY ("exciting new"); STABILITY ("established," "reputation"); SCARCITY ("limited time"); SIMPLICITY ("easy"); UTILITY ("practical").

DOWNPLAY the "bad"

▶ Ads often **omit** disadvantages such as: high cost; overpriced product or service; unwanted item - "white elephant" with little or no re-sale potential; often advice given and "secrets" are common-sense instructions, available free from books, schools, government agencies, etc.

▶ Ads often **divert** attention away from *key issues* (possible fraud) or *other choices* such as: investing time or money in other ventures which are safer, more profitable, more known.

▶ **Confusion** often occurs in the details, the very complex facts and figures; the technical, business, and legal jargon used. Many fly-by-night mail order schemes (and pyramid and chain letter schemes) simply keep the initial money sent in; Ponzi schemes delay the "sting." High risk fraud: "buyer beware!"

INTENSIFY the "good"

DOWNPLAY the "bad"

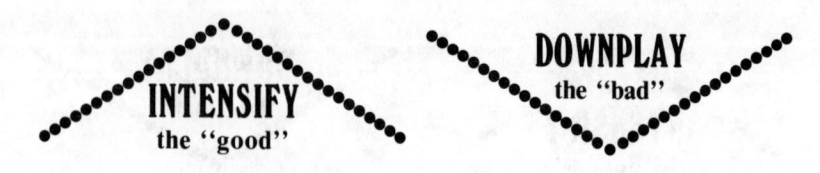

▶ Ads often **repeat** names of local real estate agents, some national networks (Century 21, Red Carpet, Gallery of Homes), local building contractors.

▶ Ads often **omit** disadvantages such as high cost, high interest rates, needed improvements, tax rates, future tax increases, zoning regulations and restrictions, lack of utilities, remote areas, no access roads, declining neighborhood; homes with hidden defects, low quality materials, inferior work, repairs needed; difficult to re-sell, not a liquid asset, etc.

▶ Ads often **associate** items with things already desired by, or held favorably by the intended audience. Human needs commonly associated here include: SURROUNDINGS ("cozy"); SECURITY ("foresight"); ECONOMY ("investment," "savings," "equity"); APPROVAL ("best people," "average people"); TERRITORY ("community," "neighborhood"); BELONGING ("family," "home"); PLAY ("recreation,"); ESTEEM ("prestigious"); GENEROSITY ("care," "share"); COMPLETION ("achieve").

▶ Ads often **divert** attention away from *other choices* such as: using the services of another agent, buying direct; renting, leasing, trading; buying lesser, or in different areas, or not buying.

▶ Ads are **composed** using key words and images intensifying the "good" of such common intrinsic qualities: SUPERIORITY ("best," "choice"); QUANTITY ("more," "roomy"); BEAUTY ("elegant," "charming"); NOVELTY ("modern," "contemporary"); STABILITY ("traditional"); SCARCITY ("rare," "unique"); SIMPLICITY ("care-free"); UTILITY ("practical").

▶ **Confusion** often occurs in the legal and technical jargon used in property contracts, in the process and procedures of a loan, a sale; title clearance. High risk fraud in certain land sales, especially in remote "scenic" areas advertised as vacation or retirement areas.

HOME REPAIRS

INTENSIFY the "good"

▶ Ads often **repeat** brand names of products (paint, tools), and local services relating to home repairs and improvements: painting, siding, roofing, rewiring, plumbing, insulation, furnace repairs, etc.

▶ Ads often **associate** items with things already desired by, or held favorably by the intended audience. Human needs commonly associated here include: SURROUNDINGS ("comfortable"); HEALTH ("beneficial"); SECURITY ("protect"); ECONOMY ("invest," "preserve"); APPROVAL ("best people," "most people,"); TERRITORY ("neighborhood"); BELONGING ("family," "friends"); PLAY ("enjoy"); ESTEEM ("admired"); GENEROSITY ("give," "share"); COMPLETION ("finish"); CREATIVITY ("make"). Common "*scare-and-sell*": dangers of fire, bad wiring.

▶ Ads are **composed** using key words and images intensifying the "good" of such common intrinsic qualities: SUPERIORITY ("best"); QUANTITY ("more"); BEAUTY ("handsome"); EFFICIENCY ("skilled"); NOVELTY ("modern"); STABILITY ("experienced," "established"); RELIABILITY ("dependable"); SCARCITY ("limited offer"); RAPIDITY ("fast"); SIMPLICITY ("convenient"); UTILITY ("practical"); SAFETY ("safe").

DOWNPLAY the "bad"

▶ Ads often **omit** disadvantages such as high total cost (installation costs, financing, etc.), inconvenience, delay, mess, inferior materials, incompetent or inexperienced workers, company not bonded or insured for accidents, effect on property taxes.

▶ Ads often **divert** attention away from *key issues* or *other choices* such as: using a competitor's services, do-it-yourself repairs, getting bids from several, moving and buying a new home, making less repairs or none at all.

▶ **Confusion** often occurs in cost estimates, expectation of finished job, conditions of time, delivery, guarantee, inspection, local building codes and restrictions. High risk fraud in dealing with fly-by-night solicitors, phony "inspectors," etc.

INTENSIFY the "good"

DOWNPLAY the "bad"

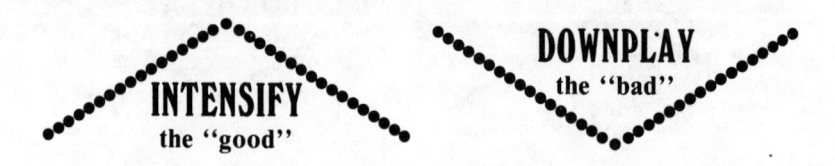

▶ Ads often **repeat** names of local dealers and national brands of *major appliances* (refrigerators, freezers, stoves, washers - Maytag, Westinghouse, Whirlpool, Frigidaire); *small appliances* (mixers, toasters - Sunbeam, General Electric, etc.); *furniture* (chairs, beds -Kroehler, Ethan Allen, Sealy, etc.)

▶ Ads often **associate** items with things already desired by, or held favorably by the intended audience. Human needs commonly associated here include: SURROUNDINGS ("comfortable"); ECONOMY ("value," "bargain," "sale"); APPROVAL ("best people," "most people"); TERRITORY ("local," "neighborhood"); BELONGING ("family"); ESTEEM ("admired," "respected"): GENEROSITY ("share," "care"); COMPLETION ("finish").

▶ Ads are **composed** using key words and images intensifying the "good" of such common intrinsic qualities: SUPERIORITY ("best"); QUANTITY ("more"); BEAUTY ("elegant," "charming"); NOVELTY ("modern"); STABILITY ("classic," "traditional"); RELIABILITY ("sturdy"); SCARCITY ("rare"); SIMPLICITY ("easy," "timesaving"); UTILITY ("practical"); SAFETY ("tested").

▶ Ads often **omit** disadvantages such as high cost, including delivery, installation, credit, repairs, parts and service; high cost-per-use (e.g. gadgets); high energy-use; limited warranty terms; overbuying (unneeded items in sets, unneeded features or "extras.")

▶ Ads often **divert** attention away from *key issues* or *other choices* such as: buying other brands of furniture and appliances; buying from other dealers; substitutes - used -furniture, buying used items, repairing own items, renting, buying less, buying less often, not buying. *"Bait and switch"* very common: ads for low-priced item to bring buyers into stores, then sellers "switch" to better, more expensive items.

▶ **Confusion** often occurs in the many varieties of styles, designs, fabrics, materials (in furniture), variety of models and features (in appliances) make it difficult to make exact comparisons; technical jargon; inflated prices and fictional "sales" and cut-prices.

UTILITIES ADS

INTENSIFY the "good"

DOWNPLAY the "bad"

▶ Ads often **repeat** names of local utilities (electric, gas, telephone) and national networks or systems (Edison, Bell, GTE, etc.). *Explicit* messages and themes, commonly stress *increased* or *more efficient* use of services (e.g. long-distance calls), *safety* suggestions (gas, electric). *Implied* advocacy messages build "good public relations" for citizen and legislative support of utilities plans, policies (e.g. nuclear power).

▶ Ads often **associate** items with things already desired by, or held favorably by the intended audience. Human needs commonly associated here include: SURROUNDINGS ("comfortable"); SECURITY ("protection"); ECONOMY ("only"); APPROVAL ("most people," "average people"); TERRITORY ("local," "community"); BELONGING ("family," "friends"); GENEROSITY ("serve," "helping").

▶ Ads are **composed** using key words and images intensifying the "good" of such common intrinsic qualities: SUPERIORITY ("best"); QUANTITY ("more"); EFFICIENCY ("capable," "helps," "solves"); NOVELTY ("modern"); STABILITY ("traditional"); RELIABILITY ("dependable"); RAPIDITY ("fast"); SIMPLICITY ("easy," "convenient"); UTILITY ("useful," "practical"); SAFETY ("protect").

▶ Ads often **omit** disadvantages such as high cost; cost of "extras" (phone styles, services); occasional or frequent poor service; customer complaints often treated with bureaucratic rudeness; policies of "investor-owned" utilities are sometimes more concerned with high profit yield than public service.

▶ Ads often **divert** attention from *key issues* (public decisions, the common good) or *other choices* such as: using the services or products of competitors (where possible), using less.

▶ **Confusion** often occurs in the many varieties of rates and services available (especially telephone); in the legal jargon concerning the conditions of the monopoly (procedures, limits, structure); in the complaint process; in the function of related governmental regulatory agencies.

INTENSIFY the "good"

▶ Ads often **repeat** names and slogans of insurance companies, including: Metropolitan, Prudential, Allstate, State Farm, Traveler's, etc.

▶ Ads often **associate** items with things already desired by, or held favorably by the intended audience. Human needs commonly associated here include: SECURITY ("protect"); APPROVAL ("most people," "average people"); TERRITORY ("hometown"); BELONGING ("family," "home"); ESTEEM ("respected"); GENEROSITY ("share" "help"); COMPLETION ("fulfill"); *"Scare-and-sell"* tactics often used, intensifying early death, accidents, disasters.

▶ Ads are **composed** using key words and images intensifying the "good" of such common intrinsic qualities: SUPERIORITY ("best"); QUANTITY ("most"); EFFICIENCY ("capable"); NOVELTY ("modern"); STABILITY ("established"); RELIABILITY ("dependable"); SIMPLICITY ("easy"); UTILITY ("practical," "sensible"); SAFETY ("certain," "sure").

DOWNPLAY the "bad"

▶ Ads often **omit** disadvantages such as high cost of some policies; age and health restrictions; exclusions within contracts; financial solvency of company.

▶ Ads often **divert** attention away from *key issues* or *other choices* such as: buying from a competitor; other forms of investing and saving; buying a less expensive policy, buying none.

▶ **Confusion** often occurs in the jargon, "small print," exclusions, limitations in policies; in the many different plans (with marginal differences) offered by competing companies, making comparison-shopping difficult; in the similarity of names used by "weak" companies posing as solvent.

INTENSIFY the "good"

DOWNPLAY the "bad"

▶ Ads often **repeat** brand names of products and services including: foods, clothes, diapers, toys, furniture, shampoos, oils, powders, etc.

▶ Ads often **associate** items with things already desired by, or held favorably by the intended audience. Human needs commonly associated here include: FOOD ("tasty"); ACTIVITY ("lively"); SURROUNDINGS ("cozy," "warm"); HEALTH ("wholesome"); SECURITY ("protect"); ECONOMY ("only"); APPROVAL ("best people," "most people"); BELONGING ("family"); PLAY ("enjoy"); ESTEEM ("admired"); GENEROSITY ("share," "care"); CURIOSITY ("learn," "educational"); COMPLETION ("achieve").

▶ Ads are **composed** using key words and images intensifying the 'good" of such common intrinsic qualities: SUPERIORITY ("best"); QUANTITY ("more"); BEAUTY ("cute"); EFFICIENCY ("really works"); NOVELTY ("modern"); STABILITY ("traditional"); RELIABILITY ("long lasting"); SCARCITY ("unique"); RAPIDITY ("fast"); SIMPLICITY ("easy"); UTILITY ("practical"); SAFETY ("childproof"). Target audience: new parents; most want to "do a good job," eager to buy, suspectible to emotional appeals.

▶ Ads often **omit** disadvantages such as high cost, limited use, health or safety hazards, basic sameness among many products.

▶ Ads often **divert** attention away from *key issues* or *other choices* such as: buying other brands, or generic products, buying substitutes (e.g. using cloth diapers); buying less, buying less often, not buying certain products or services.

▶ **Confusion** sometimes occurs in labeling (ingredients), packaging (size, weights); "specialty" sales (overpriced photography contracts, etc.).

INTENSIFY the "good"

▶ Ads often **repeat** the brand names of individual toys and games (frequently changing) and major manufacturers (Mattel, Kenner, Milton-Bradley, Parker Bros.). Alliterative songs, slogans, jingles often used, and often repeated by children.

▶ Ads often **associate** items with things already desired by, or held favorably, by the intended audience. Human needs commonly associated here include ACTIVITY ("exciting," "adventure"); ECONOMY ("only"); APPROVAL ("average people" - the gang, all the kids; frequent links with sports heroes, cartoon characters); TERRITORY ("outdoors"); BELONGING ("friends"); PLAY ("fun," "enjoy," "happy"); ESTEEM ("admired"); GENEROSITY ("give"); CURIOSITY ("discover," "educational"); CREATIVITY ("make").

▶ Ads are **composed** using key words and images intensifying the "good" of such common intrinsic qualities: SUPERIORITY ("best"); QUANTITY ("more"); BEAUTY ("cute"); EFFICIENCY ("really works"); NOVELTY ("amazing new"); RELIABILITY ("rugged," "sturdy"); SCARCITY ("collector's item"); RAPIDITY ("fast"); SIMPLICITY ("easy"); UTILITY ("all-purpose"). Target audience: children, heavy TV blitz after-school, Saturday mornings, and pre-Christmas.

DOWNPLAY the "bad"

▶ Ads often **omit** disadvantages such as high cost, limited use, too simple or too complex, fragile construction, shoddy materials, difficulty of assembly, safety hazards, psychological effects ("toy" weapons, sexist attitudes).

▶ Ads often **direct** attention away from *key issues* or *other choices* such as: buying other brands; substitutes - other activities (sports, reading, etc.); making own toys and games, buying used toys; sharing, trading, or borrowing toys and games; buying less, less often, not buying.

▶ **Confusion** often occurs in young children unable to distinquish illusion and reality, especially in TV ads in which the illusion (of fun and joy) is so hyped, so intense, that the reality is disappointing.

Reference Guide CLEANING ADS 195

INTENSIFY the "good"

DOWNPLAY the "bad"

▶ Ads often **repeat** brand names - and frequently changing slogans and jingles - including: Tide, Cheer, Bold, Gain, Dash, All, Wisk, Era, Fab, Cold Power, Ajax, Dynamo, Joy, Ivory Liquid, Palmolive, Lux, Dove, Mr. Clean, Spic n Span, Tidy Bowl, etc.

▶ Ads often **associate** items with things already desired by, or held favorably by the intended audience. Human needs commonly associated here include: ACTIVITY ("lively"); SURROUNDINGS ("fresh," "smooth"); SEX ("feminine"); HEALTH ("clean"); ECONOMY ("less"); APPROVAL ("most people," "average people"); TERRITORY ("natural"); BELONGING ("family," "friends"); ESTEEM ("admired"); GENEROSITY ("pleasing," "gratitude"); CURIOSITY ("discover"); COMPLETION ("finish").

▶ Ads are **composed** using key words and images intensifying the "good" of such common intrinsic qualities: SUPERIORITY ("best"); QUANTITY ("more"); BEAUTY ("fabulous"); EFFICIENCY ("really works"); NOVELTY ("new improved"); STABILITY ("time-tested"); RELIABILITY ("powerful"); RAPIDITY ("fast"); SIMPLICITY ("easy"); UTILITY ("practical"); SAFETY ("protects").

▶ Ads often **omit** disadvantages such as high cost (for "specialty items"); health problems (allergic reactions); safety problems (accidents, poisoning); basic sameness among brands.

▶ Ads often **divert** attention away from *key issues* or *other choices* such as: buying other brands, buying generic chemicals in bulk, buying and using less, or less often.

▶ **Confusion** often occurs in the packaging and pricing (sizes and weights), in the label language ("Economy," "Large," "Giant," "Family Size," etc.); in the vague cleaning claims.

BANK AIDS

INTENSIFY the "good"

▶ Ads often **repeat** names of local banks, and common *themes*: "friendly," "personal service," "safety" and "security." (Still a need to counter the deep distrust of moneylenders, and anti-bank feelings.) Very few big *national* ads, but banks are big spenders in *local* ads.

▶ Ads often **associate** items with things already desired by, or held favorably by the intended audience. Human needs commonly associated here include: SECURITY ("safeguard"); ECONOMY ("earn," "invest," "save"); APPROVAL ("best people," "most people," "average people"); TERRITORY ("local," "hometown"); BELONGING ("friendly"); ESTEEM ("respected," "influential"); COMPLETION ("achieve").

▶ Ads are **composed** using key words and images intensifying the "good" of such common intrinsic qualities: SUPERIORITY ("best"); QUANTITY ("more services"); EFFICIENCY ("capable"); NOVELTY ("modern"); STABILITY ("established"); RELIABILITY ("dependable"); SIMPLICITY ("convenient"); UTILITY ("practical"); SAFETY ("insured").

DOWNPLAY the "bad"

▶ Ads often **omit** disadvantages such as cost of loans; cost of services; time and location often inconvenient; "personal attention" often not a reality; banks downplay their *power* as a mortgage-holder or lien-holder.

▶ Ads often **divert** attention from *key issues* (banks profit by stimulating consumer debts) or *other choices* such as: banking with competitors; using Savings and Loans, or non-profit Credit Unions; investing and saving in stocks, real estate; borrowing less money, etc.

▶ **Confusion** often occurs in the jargon of the banking industry; in statistics, interest rates, credit terms, "free gift" premiums, service costs, etc. Despite confusing claims about "highest" rates for savings, federal and state laws regulate most banking transactions.

INTENSIFY
the "good"

DOWNPLAY
the "bad"

▶ Ads often **repeat** names of credit cards from banks, travel companies, major stores and oil companies including: Master Charge, Visa, American Express, Diner's Club, Carte Blanche, Sears, Wards, Amoco, etc.

▶ Ads often **associate** items with things already desired by, or held favorably by the intended audience. Human needs commonly associated here include: ACTIVITY ("lively"); SECURITY ("protect"); ECONOMY ("less than"); APPROVAL ("best people," "most people"); TERRITORY ("local"); BELONGING ("family," "friends"); PLAY ("enjoy"); ESTEEM ("respected"); GENEROSITY ("delight"); CURIOUSITY ("discover"); COMPLETION ("achieve").

▶ Ads are **composed** using key words and images intensifying the "good" of such common intrinsic qualities: SUPERIORITY ("best"); QUANTITY ('most"); EFFICIENCY ("really works"); NOVELTY ("modern"); STABILITY ("established"); RELIABILITY ("dependable"); SCARCITY ("exclusive"); RAPIDITY ("instant"); SIMPLICITY ("easy"); UTILITY ("practical", "use anywhere"); SAFETY ("protection").

▶ Ads **omit** disadvantages such as high interest cost (usually 18% - 21%); with some, membership fee; ease of getting into a debt cycle; responsibility for lost or stolen cards.

▶ Ads **divert** attention away from *key issues* (debt cycle), or *other choices* such as: using other credit cards, borrowing at lower interest from banks or credit unions, saving in advance, using the card less often, for lesser amounts, or not at all.

▶ **Confusion** often occurs in the language, legal jargon on billing statements; interest charges; if "country-club" billing isn't used, no receipts are available; often difficult to have errors corrected on computer statements. EFT and "debit" cards differ from traditional credit cards.

FUNERAL ADS

INTENSIFY the "good"

▶ Ads often **repeat** names of local funeral homes, and common *themes*: "service," "care," "concern." Most advertising is indirect "public relations" such as "donations" and "contributions" to church bulletins, calendars, local clubs, schools, etc.

▶ Ads often **associate** items with things already desired by, or held favorably by the intended audience. Human needs commonly associated here include: ACTIVITY ("peaceful"); SECURITY ("protect"); ECONOMY ("reasonable"); APPROVAL ("religious"); TERRITORY ("neighborhood"); BELONGING ("family," "friends"); ESTEEM ("honored," "respected"); GENEROSITY ("loved one," "care"); COMPLETION ("finish").

▶ Ads are **composed** using key words and images intensifying the "good" of such common intrinsic qualities: SUPERIORITY ("best"); QUANTITY ("more"); BEAUTY ("tasteful"); EFFICIENCY ("competant"); NOVELTY ("modern"); STABILITY ("traditional"); RELIABILITY ("sturdy"); SCARCITY ("rare"); SIMPLICITY ("all-included"); UTILITY ("practical"); SAFETY ("withstands"). Target audience: families of people who die; such buyers often rushed, under emotional stress, unable to "shop" deliberately.

DOWNPLAY the "bad"

▶ Ads often **omit** disadvantages such as frequent consumer complaints (and FTC action) about "pressure" tactics to sell unnecessary or expensive services to emotionally-distressed family members; often embalming is *not* required, nor special vaults.

▶ Ads often **divert** attention away from *key issues* (necessity) or *other choices* such as: using a competitor's services; joining a non-profit burial society; buying less expensive services (e.g. *renting* a display coffin for the wake); cremation; "pre-need" planning and arrangements.

▶ **Confusion** often occurs in the cost and variety of service "packages"; in legal and technical jargon used; misleading statements about legal, religious, and cemetary requirements. (Unsolicited mail often arrives after deaths - selling "memorial" items or begging money.)

U.S. Advertising Expenditures

Advertising Age, the industry's major newspaper, each September publishes an overview of advertising statistics. Basic data, together with commentary and analysis, is presented in a series of marketing reports organized by **company** ("100 Leading National Advertisers"), by **industry** (airlines, food, soaps, etc.), and by **media** (TV, radio, newspaper, outdoor, etc.). The samples below are reprinted with permission from the Sept. 10 and Sept. 14, 1981 issues of *Advertising Age.* Copyright 1981 by Crain Communications, Inc.

10 Leading National Advertisers	(Total Ad Dollars in Millions-1980)
1. Proctor & Gamble Co.	$649.6
2. Sears, Roebuck & Co.	$599.6
3. General Foods Corp.	$410.0
4. Philip Morris Inc.	$364.6
5. K mart Corp.	$319.3
6. General Motors Corp.	$316.0
7. R. J. Reynolds Industries	$298.5
8. Ford Motor Co.	$280.0
9. American Telephone & Telegraph	$259.2
10. Warner-Lambert Co.	$235.2

Advertising Expenditures
(by Media - Total Ad Dollars in Millions - 1980)

Newspaper	15,541
Magazines	3,149
Farm publications	130
TV	11,366
Radio	3,777
Direct mail	7,596
Business paper	1,674
Outdoor	600
Misc.	10,767
TOTAL	54,600

U.S. Advertising Expenditures

(Total Ad Dollars in Billions)

Year	
1935	1.7
1940	2.1
1950	5.7
1960	11.9
1961	11.8
1962	12.4
1963	13.1
1964	14.1
1965	15.2
1966	16.6
1967	16.8
1968	18.0
1969	19.4
1970	19.5
1971	20.7
1972	23.3
1973	25.1
1974	26.8
1975	28.1
1976	33.6
1977	37.9
1978	43.9
1979	49.5
1980	54.6
1981	61.6

ABOUT THE AUTHOR

HUGH RANK is a Professor of English at Governors State University, Park Forest South, Illinois. Educated at the University of Notre Dame (B.A., M.A., Ph.D.), he has previously taught at Arizona State University, Sacred Heart University (Connecticut), Saint Joseph's College (Indiana), and as a Fulbright Professor (Copenhagen, Denmark). He has also served as a Public Information Officer in the U.S. Army (Germany).

In 1972, he became the first Chairman of the Committee on Public Doublespeak, of the National Council of Teachers of English (NCTE), a group with which he has worked now for over a decade. He has edited *Language and Public Policy* (NCTE, 1974) and has been a frequent contributor to the academic journals. In 1976, he released the "Intensify/Downplay Schema" (reprinted here) as a new way of teaching propaganda analysis; in that year his colleagues awarded him the George Orwell Award *"for distinquished contribution toward honesty and clarity in public language."* In 1982, he released the "30-Second-Spot-Quiz" (reprinted here) as another simple teaching device useful to analyze persuasion.

INDEX

acquisition 46
"added value" associations
  activity 84
  completion 128
  creativity 126
  curiosity 124
  economy 94
  elite 100
  esteem 118
  family 114
  food 82
  generosity 122
  groups 116
  health 90
  intimacy 112
  nation 108
  nature 110
  neighborhood 106
  normality 104
  play 120
  popularity 102
  religion 96
  science 98
  security 92
  sex 88
  surroundings 86
AIDA formula 17
Aristotle 31
association 75, 152, 156
attention-getting 19

audience ... 42
authority figure ... 36
"bandwagon" ... 102
benefit-seeking ... 43
brand names ... 38
carpe diem ... 134
claims, most repeated ... 74
command propaganda ... 134
composition ... 152, 156
conditioning propaganda ... 134
confidence-building ... 31
conflicts ... 80
confusion ... 153, 155
consequences ... 15
coupons ... 144
counter-propaganda ... 12
deception ... 37
degree ... 78, 81
desire-stimulating ... 41
direct mail ... 144
diversion ... 153, 155
dominant impression ... 150
"doublespeak" committee ... 146, 153, 203
election rhetoric ... 34
endorsers ... 36
Establishment rhetoric ... 46
ethos ... 31
fears ... 81
flag-waving ... 108
friend figures ... 36
frustrations ... 80
Fulbright, Sen. Wm. ... 10
"glittering generalities" ... 50
"hard sell" ... 133, 137
"hidden persuaders" ... 15
image-building ... 31
impulse buying ... 142
inequality ... 10, 12, 78
Intensify/Downplay schema ... 151
intrinsic qualities, claims:
    beauty ... 54
    efficiency ... 56
    novelty ... 60
    quantity ... 52
    rapidity ... 70
    reliability ... 64
    safety ... 72
    scarcity ... 58
    simplicity ... 66
    stability ... 62
    superiority ... 50
    utility ... 68
"main selling point" ... 43
market research ... 75
Maslow, A. ... 43
Monroe's Motivated Sequence ... 17
N.C.T.E. ... 146, 151, 203
Nielsen ratings ... 102
omission ... 153, 155
"plain folks" ... 104
"plastic people" ... 37
polls ... 102
prevention ... 47
Price, J. ... 145
product-oriented ... 42

Index

products and services:
- airlines . . . 181
- appliances . . . 190
- automobiles . . . 173
- baby care . . . 193
- banks . . . 196
- beer . . . 161
- "body work" . . . 170
- candy . . . 164
- cameras . . . 176
- cars . . . 173
- car care . . . 174
- cereals . . . 165
- cigarettes . . . 163
- cleaning aids . . . 195
- clothes . . . 172
- colleges . . . 183
- cosmetics . . . 171
- credit cards . . . 197
- cycles . . . 175
- easy-foods . . . 167
- entertainments . . . 179
- fast-foods . . . 168
- funerals . . . 198
- furniture . . . 190
- get-rich-quick schemes . . . 187
- homes . . . 188
- home repairs . . . 189
- hotels . . . 180
- insurance . . . 192
- job ads . . . 184
- liquor . . . 162
- LP records . . . 178
- military . . . 182
- motels . . . 180
- motorcycles . . . 175
- O-T-C drugs . . . 169
- real estate . . . 188
- self-improvement . . . 186
- snack foods . . . 166
- soft drinks . . . 160
- stereos . . . 177
- toys . . . 194
- utilities . . . 191
- weddings . . . 185

propaganda . . . 9, 134
protection . . . 46
puffery . . . 50
"Questions You Can Ask . . ." . . . 155
reform rhetoric . . . 46
relief . . . 46
repitition . . . 152, 156
response . . . 141
Riesman, D. . . . 102
"scare-and-sell" . . . 49, 81
"soft sell" . . . 133
standard phrasing . . . 130
"sublimal seduction" . . . 15
Swann, C. . . . 10
sweepstakes . . . 144
telephone . . . 144
testimonials . . . 36
"30-Second-Spot Quiz" . . . 147
trademarks . . . 38
urgency . . . 133
Young, J. . . . 28